Playing the Whore

The Jacobin series features short interrogations of politics, economics, and culture from a socialist perspective, as an avenue to radical political practice. The books offer critical analysis and engagement with the history and ideas of the Left in an accessible format.

The series is a collaboration between Verso Books and *Jacobin* magazine, which is published quarterly in print and online at jacobinmag.com.

Other titles in this series available from Verso Books:

Utopia or Bust by Benjamin Kunkel
Strike for America by Micah Uetricht

Playing the Whore

The Work of Sex Work

by
MELISSA GIRA GRANT

VERSO

London • New York

First published by Verso 2014
© Melissa Gira Grant 2014

1 3 5 7 9 10 8 6 4 2

Verso
UK: 6 Meard Street, London W1F 0EG
US: 20 Jay Street, Suite 1010, Brooklyn, NY 11201
www.versobooks.com

Verso is the imprint of New Left Books

ISBN-13: 978-1-78168-323-1
eISBN-13: 978-1-78168-324-8 (US)
eISBN-13: 978-1-78168-638-6 (UK)

British Library Cataloguing in Publication Data
A catalogue record for this book is available from the British Library

Library of Congress Cataloging-in-Publication Data
A catalog record for this book is available from the Library of Congress

Typeset in Fournier MT by Hewer Text UK Ltd, Edinburgh
Printed in the US by Maple Press

Archange ou putain
Je veux bien
Tous les rôles
me sont prêtés . . .

Archangel or whore
I don't mind
All the roles
are lent to me . . .

—Colette Peignot (Laure)
Le Sacré, trans. Barbara Ann Brown

Contents

1

The Police

"An attractive blonde walks into a Fargo hotel room," it begins, "followed by a mustached man in a black leather jacket. He asks what brought her to town." The blonde in the low-slung jeans is about to sit down. You can just see her shoulder and the back of her head.

In another room, a man looks at a woman with long dark hair. She's seated across from him, wrapped in a robe or a shirt. It's hard to see in the glare of the bedside lamp. He stands and slips off his boxers. He asks if she would let him see hers. She drops the robe or the shirt from her shoulders a few inches, then excuses herself to go freshen up.

"You'll be satisfied," a third woman says. "This is my job."

There's always a television, and it's playing a western, or the kind of old Hollywood picture with men dancing in topcoats and tails. In front of the flat screen, two women are cuffed. He's ordered them to sit for questioning.

As he reaches for one of the women's wrists, the man in the cop uniform says, "We're just going to lock these cuffs, so they don't get tight on you." She asks, "Can I ask what I did wrong?"

"I'm not gon[na] lie," writes a commenter under one of the videos, ". . . i jacked off to this."

Though they resemble amateur pornography's opening shots, you will not find these videos by searching YouPorn, PornHub, or RedTube. They're published at JohnTV.com, which boasts "over sixty million views." JohnTV is the project of "Video Vigilante" Brian Bates, who since 1996 has been trailing women he suspects to be "prostitutes" and "hookers" and shoots videos of them with men he tells us are their "johns."

JohnTV posts are sorted into sections: Busts, Stings, and Pimp Profiles. These start with a mug shot—usually of a black man—followed by his name and criminal allegations. Bates claims he "often works with patrol officers" and members of the "Vice Unit on cases involving human trafficking." He also goes solo, trailing people on streets, in parked cars, wherever he finds people he considers suspicious, attempting to catch men in the act and the women with them. For Bates, the camera isn't just a tool for producing evidence: It's his cover for harassing women he believes are selling sex, pinning a record on them online even when the law will not.

Bates didn't shoot the six videos from Fargo. "This is the first time JohnTV has come across videos of this sort," he gushes on his blog. "Usually these sorts of videos only appear on television after being highly edited by television programs such as *COPS*." These six unedited videos are embeds from a North Dakota news outlet, where they ran with the headline, "Watch Local Prostitution Stings Unfold." But they weren't produced by reporters. The videos were created by the Fargo Police Department.

There's so much to watch in the long minutes between negotiation and interrogation, and it repeats—the nervous customer asking if he's going to get "full service" or if she "upsells," the undercovers' rehearsed excuses that they "just need, like, a five-minute shower" while they call for backup, then the sudden, crashing appearance of black vests and ball caps and guns drawn on undressed people, who are told to bend and kneel and spread their arms.

Prostitution stings are a law enforcement tactic used to target men who buy sex and women who sell it—or men and women who the police have profiled in this way. These days, rather than limit their patrol to the street, vice cops search the Web for advertisements they believe offer sex for sale, contact the advertisers while posing as customers, arrange hotel meetings, and attempt to make an arrest from within the relative comfort of a room with free Wi-Fi and an ice machine down the hall.

Whether these videos are locked in an evidence room, broadcast on the eleven o'clock news, or blogged by a vigilante, they are themselves a punishment. We could arrest you at any time, they say. Even if no one is there to witness your arrest, everyone will know. When we record your arrest, when you're viewed again and again, you will be getting arrested all the time.

In the United States, one of the last industrialized nations which continues to outlaw sex for sale, we must ask: Why do we insist that there is a public good in staging sex transactions to make arrests? Is the point to produce order, to protect, or to punish?

No evidence will be weighed before the arrest video is published. Even if she was not one before, in the eyes of the viewer and in the memory of search engines, this woman is now a prostitute. As so few people arrested for prostitution-related offenses fight their charges, there is no future event to displace the arrest video, to restate that those caught on tape didn't, as one of the women arrested in Fargo said, "do anything wrong." The undercover police, perpetually arresting in these videos, enact a form of sustained violence on these women's bodies. Even with a camera, it is not immediately visible.

To produce a prostitute where before there had been only a woman is the purpose of such policing. It is a socially acceptable way to discipline women, fueled by a lust for law and order that is at the core of what I call the "prostitute imaginary"—the ways in which we conceptualize and make arguments about prostitution. The prostitute imaginary compels those who seek to control, abolish, or otherwise profit from prostitution, and is also the rhetorical product of their efforts. It is driven by both fantasies and fears about sex and the value of human life.

The sting itself, aside from the unjust laws it enforces, or the trial that may never result, is intended to incite fear. These stings form just one part of a matrix of widespread police misconduct toward sex workers and people profiled as sex workers. In New York City, for example, 70 percent of sex workers working outdoors surveyed by the Sex Workers Project reported near daily run-ins with police, and 30 percent reported being threatened with violence. According to "The Revolving Door: An Analysis of Street-Based Prostitution in New York City," when street-based sex workers sought help from the police, they were often ignored.

> Carol told researchers, "If I call them, they don't come. If I have a situation in the street, forget it. 'Nobody told you to be in the street.' After a girl was gang-raped, they said, 'Forget it, she works in the street.' She said, 'I hope that never happens to your daughters. I'm human.'"
>
> Jamie had an incident where she was "hanging out on the stroll . . . these guys in a jeep driving by . . . one guy in a car threw a bottle at me . . . I went to the cops [who told me] we didn't have a right being in that area because we know it's a prostitution area, and whatever came our way, we deserved it."

Police violence isn't limited to sex workers who work outdoors. In a parallel survey conducted by the Sex Workers Project, 14 percent of those who primarily work indoors reported that police had been violent toward them; 16 percent reported that police officers had initiated a sexual interaction.

This was in New York City, where the police department is notorious for violating civil rights in the course of law enforcement, but look globally, where violations of sex workers' rights by police are also common—and well documented. In West Bengal, the sex worker collective Durbar Mahila Samanwaya Committee surveyed over 21,000 women who do sex work.

They collected 48,000 reports of abuse or violence by police—in contrast with 4,000 reports of violence by customers, who are conventionally thought of as the biggest threat to sex workers, especially by campaigners opposed to prostitution.

Police violence against sex workers is a persistent global reality. As the economy collapsed in Greece, police staged raids on brothels, arrested and detained sex workers, forced them to undergo HIV testing, and released their photos and HIV status to the media. These actions were condemned by UNAIDS and Human Rights Watch. In China, police have forced sex workers they have arrested to walk in "shame parades," public processions in which they are shackled and then photographed. Police published these photos on the Web, including one in which a cop humiliated a nude sex worker by pulling her hair back and brutally exposing her face to the camera. When the photo went viral, the outcry reportedly prompted police to suspend these public shaming rituals, though they continue to make violent arrests and raids.

One could hope that the photos and videos like these could make the pervasiveness of this violence real to the public. But to truly confront this type of violence would require us to admit that we permit some violence against women to be committed in order to protect the social and sexual value of other women.

Violence's Value

I've stopped asking, Why have we made prostitution illegal? Instead I want an explanation for, How much violence against "prostitutes" have we made acceptable? The police run-ins, the police denying help, the police abuse—all this shapes the context in which the sting, and the video of it, form a complete pursuit of what we are to understand as justice, which in this case is limited to some form of punishment, of acceptable violence.

As I was working on this book I was invited to give a presentation to law students and fellows at Yale University. In my talk, I described these videos. Afterward, as I stood in the door about to leave, several students approached me individually to say that they thought my presentation would have been more persuasive if I had prefaced it by stating my "position on prostitution."

"Do you need to know if I oppose prostitution," I asked these students, "before you can evaluate how you feel about police abuse, about a persistent pattern of denying justice to people labeled 'prostitutes'?" Are these videos to be understood only as documents of an acceptable form of violence, to be applied as a deterrent, to deliberately make prostitution less safe?

My presentation remains, with this addendum: these students taught me to see how narrowly and insistently people can focus their opposition to what they understand as "the system" of prostitution, so much so that even police violence against sex workers is collapsed into that system, how this violence appears inevitable. The stigma and violence faced by sex workers are far greater harms than sex work itself, yet this is illegible to those who only see prostitution as a self-enforcing system of violence. For them, prostitution marks out the far reach of what's acceptable for women and men, where rights end and violence is justice. This is accepted as the cost of protecting those most deserving of protection. Opponents of sex work decry prostitution as a violent institution, yet concede that violence is also useful to keep people from it.

The Fargo videos invite the public to witness this violence against sex workers, a criteria we don't admit to using to define their existence. Here we see evidence of their lives only as they are put on display the last critical minutes of a police tactic meant to exert control over sex workers' abilities to move in public spaces, to make a living, to determine the conditions of their labor. These videos capture and relay the moment—an agreement made and money exchanged—that is nearly universally understood as defining prostitution, though it is also marked here with the particulars of the indoor, Internet-powered sex trade: Two people going behind closed doors, seated on floral bedcovers, and counting bills before getting down to business—and before the cuffs go on. In the prevailing view, this is the moment to which nearly all sex workers' lives are reduced.

As seen from a motel room in Fargo, North Dakota, those lives are worth comparatively little to the public until they pass in front of the policeman's camera.

The Carceral Eye

This is the social act to which the prostitute is reduced: the moment cash is handed to her; the moment she makes an agreement. It's not a coincidence that this is what the law is most concerned with. In most cases, it's not necessary for police to observe a sex act in progress in order to make an arrest. In fact, in some countries, like Canada and the UK, the sex act itself is not illegal. What is illegal in many jurisdictions is the "communication for the purposes of . . . solicitation" or even, "loitering with intent to solicit."

Prostitution is, much of the time, a talking crime.

In some cities, it's a walking crime. In Washington, DC, cops have the leeway to arrest people congregating in groups of two or more if they are doing so in areas decreed by the chief of police as "prostitution free zones." In Queens, New York, transgender women report in significant numbers that they cannot walk freely in their own neighborhoods—from their apartments, to the train—without being followed by cops, who accuse them of being out "working"—whether they are or not. "I was just buying tacos," a transgender Latina woman from Jackson Heights told Make the Road New York. "They grabbed me and handcuffed me. They found condoms in my bra and said I was doing sex work. After handcuffing me they asked me to kneel down and they took my wig off. They arrested me and took me away."

Sex workers and anyone perceived to be a sex worker are believed to *always* be working, or, in the cops' view, always committing a crime. People who are profiled by cops as sex workers include, in disproportionate numbers, trans women, women of color, and queer and gender nonconforming youth. This isn't about policing sex. It's about profiling and policing people whose sexuality and gender are considered suspect.

It's not just that police need to appear "tough on crime," to follow orders and keep certain people off the streets through harassment, profiling, and arrests. Appeals for stepped-up vice enforcement come not just from command but from feminist corners, too. Take the relatively recent swing in antiprostitution rhetoric, the assertions of even mainstream women's rights organizations that rather than arrest those they call "prostituted women," police ought to arrest "the johns," "the demand." This is how we find the National Organization for Women and Equality Now on the same side as those who commit violence against sex workers: cops . . . This is how we come to have a female prosecutor such as New York's Nassau County district attorney Kathleen Rice celebrating the arrest of 106 men for allegedly buying sex in a single month—and leaving out of her press conference the arrests in that same month sex of twenty-three women for allegedly selling sex, omitting their mug shots from the blown-up poster board that was at her side in front of the news cameras. Women are still getting arrested in the course of busting johns.

District Attorney Rice is a near perfect model of what sociologist Elizabeth Bernstein describes as "carceral feminism," a reliance on the law-and-order power of the state to bring about gender justice. Rather than couching crackdowns on sex work as fighting crime, now some feminists appeal to the police to pursue stings against the sex trade in the name of gender equality. We can't arrest our way to feminist utopia, but that has not stopped influential women's rights organizations from demanding that we try.

This is how District Attorney Rice is able to claim that

when she arrests men she is "going after the demand," but when she arrests women she is only "getting them into services." How, exactly, is someone who is most used to having the police threaten them, or demand sex with them in exchange for not being arrested, then supposed to trust the police in any way, let alone to connect them to services which are already freely available? Is it that impossible to imagine there is a better party for reaching out to sex workers than the police? Have we so internalized law enforcement as the go-betweens, the regulators, and the bosses of sex workers that we can't imagine prostitution without them?

We are using the policeman's eye when we can't see a sex worker as anything but his or her work, as an object to control. It's not just a carceral eye; it's a sexual eye. If a sex worker is always working, always available, she (with this eye, almost always a she) is essentially sexual. It's the eye of the hotel room surveillance video but applied to our neighborhoods, our community groups, and our policies. Even the most seemingly benign "rehabilitation" programs for sex workers are designed to isolate them from the rest of the population. They may be described as shelters, but the doors are locked, the phones are monitored, and guests are forbidden. When we construct help in this way we use the same eye with which we build and fill prisons. This isn't compassion. This isn't charity. This is control.

When we look at sex workers this way we produce conditions in which they are always being policed. "Criminalization" isn't just a law on the books but a state of being and moving in the world, of forming relationships—of having them predetermined for you. This is why we demonize the customer's perspective on the sex worker as one of absolute control, why we situate the real violence sex workers can face as the individual man's responsibility, and why we imagine that all sex workers must be powerless to say no. We have no way of understanding how to relate to the prostitute we've imagined *but* through control.

This fixation on control is what constrains our vision of sex work just as much as sex work's clandestine nature. I want to remove these constraints and move beyond the imaginary. What follows is not a promise of some new reality beyond the fantasy for hire that sex workers engage in but the slow circling around of a more persistent fantasy, and its end.

2

The Prostitute

I challenge you to distinguish a naked prostitute from any other naked woman.

—Henri Leclerc, attorney representing
Dominique Strauss-Kahn (2011)

Controlling the sale of sex is not as timeless as we might imagine it to be. Commercial sex—as a practice and an industry—as well as the class of people within it are continuously being reinvented. So many methods of punishing what's thought of as sexual deviance persist, imprisoning "sodomites" and "fallen women," for example, even as the names we give these dangerous characters shift with time. Some say the danger began to drain out when the outcast whore gave way to the victimized prostitute at the end of the nineteenth century; since the middle of the seventies, "prostitution" has slowly begun to give way to "sex work." It's this transition from a state of being to a form of labor that must be understood if we're to understand demands that sex work is work: how it came along; what goals it serves; who drove it; who contests it; who it benefits. The most important difference is that the designation of sex work is the invention of the people who perform it.

This is why I'm not so interested in what people think of prostitution: It doesn't really exist anymore. The person we call "the prostitute," contrary to her honorific as a member of "the world's oldest profession," hasn't actually been around very long. The word is young, and at first it didn't confer identity. When *prostitute* entered into English in the sixteenth century it was as a verb—*to prostitute*, to set something up for sale.

The word *whore* is older, old English or old German, possibly derived from a root that's no longer known, and dates back as early as the twelfth century BCE. There were countless people whose lives prior to the word's invention were later reduced by historians to the word *whore*, though their activities certainly varied. Contrary to King James, there was no whore of Babylon. There were no prostitutes in Pompeii. No one, not in old or new Amsterdam, worked in a red-light district until they were named as such toward the end of the nineteenth century.

It's the nineteenth century that brings us the person of the prostitute, who we are to understand was a product of the institution that came to be known as prostitution but was actually born of something much broader. Prior to this period, anthropologist Laura Agustín explains in *Sex at the Margins*, there was no word or concept which signified exclusively the sale of sexual services ... "Whoring" referred to sexual relations outside of marriage and connoted immorality or promiscuity without the involvement of money, and the word "whore" was used to brand any woman who stepped out of current boundaries of respectability.

At the same time that we see a new kind of woman in the character of the prostitute, we also see the invention of a new kind of man, the homosexual. But just as sexual relations between people of the same gender of course preceded him as constructed in this period, so too was the identity of the prostitute applied to a much older set of practices, and for parallel purposes: to produce a person by transforming a behavior (however occasional) into an identity. From there a class was marked that could now be more easily imagined, located, treated, and controlled by law. This is the character laws are made for: a fantasy of absolute degradation who is abandoned by all but those noble few who seek to rescue her.

And—to the dismay of prostitutes and homosexuals, and to those of us who are both—we have not left this period. The late nineteenth century made criminals of the people, not just of the practices of sodomy and the sale of sex. In the late twentieth century, outsized forms of AIDS led to the levy of social and criminal penalties against these same people. These penalties were not against *all* people who engaged in same-sex sex or in selling sex but against those who were most visibly different and most easily associated with other forms of deviance.

We would be wise to remember that the raid on the Stonewall Inn one June night in 1969 would not have become a police riot were it not for the street-hustling transvestites (as they then referred to themselves) who resisted when threatened with arrest, who tossed coins and bottles back at the police. Still, the same people, the queens and the butches and the hustlers who kicked off gay liberation's most celebrated battle—one that has so surely and safely ascended the ranks of civil rights history that it found its way into President Barack Obama's second inaugural address—are those most likely to experience police harassment in the neighborhood around Stonewall to this day.

We—and especially people who sell sex—have not yet fully departed from this period.

I was born in the same year and in the same country in which sex work was invented. "In 1978," writes Carol Leigh, a sex worker activist, artist, and author, in her essay "Inventing Sex Work,"

> I attended a conference in San Francisco organized by Women Against Violence in Pornography and Media. This conference was part of a weekend of activism featuring Andrea Dworkin and an anti-porn march through North Beach, San Francisco's "adult entertainment district," during which the marchers embarrassed and harassed the strippers and other sex industry workers in the neighborhood.

A march like this could only be construed as a feminist activity if they believed that the people they targeted had in some way directed or requested such a protest. They would have to conclude that these marches were somehow distinguishable, to those workers, from the vice raids that targeted the same businesses—their workplaces—that the marchers were protesting against. Or the marchers would have to tell themselves that they simply knew—better than the sex workers—what was in their best interests.

Carol Leigh understood that by attending this conference as a prostitute she could confound some of these assumed divisions within feminism—that the prostitute who would be discussed in the conference room would herself be absent. This presumption was a profound departure from the prevailing feminist theory of the day: Politics proceed from women's own experiences. Which women, though? Women in the sex trades were not the first to challenge their presupposed absence (for not being out) and simultaneous inclusion (for being part of the universal class of women) in a largely white, cisgender, middle-class, and heterosexual room of their own.

People who sell sex, and the women who sell sex in particular, are not absent from these rooms, and as Carol Leigh attests, themselves bear witness to the politics of exclusion perpetuated by other women who don't understand that they share sex workers' concerns. "I found the room for the conference workshop on prostitution," she continues,

> As I entered I saw a newsprint pad with the title of the workshop. It included the phrase "Sex Use Industry." The words stuck out and embarrassed me. How could I sit

amid other women as a political equal when I was being objectified like that, described only as something used, obscuring my role as an actor and agent in this transaction? At the beginning of the workshop I suggested that the title of the workshop should be changed to the "Sex Work Industry," because that described what women did. Generally, the men used the services, and the women provided them. As I recall, no one raised objections.

Carol Leigh realized that she had not been alone. "One woman, another writer and performer, came up to me after the workshop to tell me that she had been a prostitute as a teenager," recalls Leigh, "but was unable to discuss it for fear of being condemned."

As women lined up at conferences like these in the second wave of feminism to demolish caricatures of female subservience—the innocent daughter, the selfless wife—the wretched prostitute is one myth they refused to denounce entirely. Even "compassionate" feminists like Kate Millett, herself in attendance as prostitutes crashed another, earlier women's conference in New York, wrote of them somewhat sympathetically in *The Prostitution Papers*. However she "failed to understand the issue," writes historian Melinda Chateauvert. Millet believed "that the prostitute's 'problem' (as she saw it) could be solved by 'some fundamental reorientation in the self-image of the prostitute,' [that] prostitutes could be rehabilitated through feminist consciousness-raising." That sex workers might be capable of doing this on their own, without guidance from their sisters, that their demands might extend to far beyond "self-image," was still unimaginable.

A Politics of Sex Work

It's impossible to come to a politics of sex work without referring back to the prostitutes and the whores who came before them, all the characters who populate the prostitute imaginary. This explains why the politics of sex work are persistently framed as a woman's issue, though not all people who do sex work are women. Men are only present as pimps or johns or, more recently though no less problematically, as buyers and, strangely, not simply as customers or clients—perhaps because sex workers prefer these terms. When women in the sex trade are imagined, they are presented as objects of those men's desires or violence. Men who work in the sex trade are rarely considered members of the same occupation.

Transgender women who sell sex are presented in media accounts only in stereotype, and they often aren't understood even by sympathetic campaigners in relationship to other women in the sex trade. While there has also been a long history of gender nonconformity in the industry, it being one reliably available form of income for people who face discrimination in other forms of employment, gender nonconforming people in the sex trade are nearly invisible to those outside sex work. Anti-sex work feminists, meanwhile, don't see sex work as a place for any woman. It is telling that many feminists who wish to abolish all forms of sex work, like *The Transsexual Empire* author Janice Raymond and author of *The Industrial Vagina* Sheila Jeffreys, refuse to accept that trans women are women. They appear to believe that those engaged in sex work are not yet capable of being real women.

What we should also bear in mind when considering any study or news story that purports to examine prostitutes or prostitution is that many who are described with these terms do not use them to describe themselves. When many researchers and reporters go looking for prostitutes, they find only those who conform to their stereotypes, since they are the only people the searchers think to look for. If sex workers defy those stereotypes, that is treated as a trivial novelty rather than reality.

Even today, in the course of their work it is uncommon for sex workers to refer to themselves as such with their customers. Sex work is a political identity, one that has not fully replaced the earlier identifications imposed upon them. Phrases such as "sex worker" and "people in the sex trade" are used here, the better to describe all of the people who sell or trade sex or sexual services. "Prostitute" appears primarily to refer to its historical use; if I am speaking of someone in the sex trade in a period before the phrase "sex work" was invented, I will most likely not use it. In contemporary contexts, I will use the words "prostitute" and "prostitution" when they are used by others; for example, by those who describe themselves as prostitutes or who describe their politics as antiprostitution.

Use of the phrase "sex work," then, like those that preceded it, is unevenly and politically distributed. Sex workers may be referred to in the literature of public health, for example, but that is due to their own advocacy, and in particular of those who pushed back early in the AIDS era against the notion that prostitutes were responsible for the illness, an update of earlier health panics—syphilis, VD—in which many saw the bodies of prostitutes being considered little more than "vectors of disease." Outside of sex workers' own political networks, the shift to "sex work" is most complete in the world of AIDS, at least linguistically, though in putting policy and funding into action, fights do remain. The production of sex work has not gone without significant and persistent contest.

Sex workers can be found taking up the most public space within their own cultural production: ads, Web sites, photos, videos. Here's where sex workers are most directly involved in creating their own images, informed by competing needs for exposure and discretion. Confined to media channels that haven't censored them outright, this media is meant for customers. It would be a mistake to read such advertisements and other marketing as complete representations of sex workers. They are not meant to convey life off the clock.

This hasn't stopped antiprostitution social reformers from using them as evidence of the conditions of sexual labor. They don't understand such marketing as intentionally glamorized, even as the so-called glamorization of sex work is something that greatly concerns these campaigners in other forms of media. (Responsible for making sex work attractive to potential sex workers, according to antiprostitution activists: the movie *Pretty Woman*, the television show *Secret Diary of a Call Girl*, and what they call "pimp culture" in hip-hop. Not as responsible, apparently, are: the labor market, the privatization of education and healthcare, and debt.) All their emphasis on the pop culture depiction of the prostitute allows those opposed to sex work to keep their fight within the realm of the representational.

For a time it felt as if the fight might not be a long one: In the United States in the early seventies, sympathetic portraits of prostitutes entered the mainstream alongside an increased visibility of commercial sex as part of city life and tourism. It was 1971 when Jane Fonda took home an Oscar for her role as a bohemian, independent call girl in *Klute*, and a firsthand account of prostitution, *The Happy Hooker*, arrived on the *New York Times* bestseller list the following year. Also at the opening of the decade, after a series of court rulings appeared to relax prohibitions on "obscenity," the cities of Boston and Detroit became the first in the nation to explore licensing adult entertainment businesses. Times Square, then the most cinematic red-light district in the world, had not yet completely expelled them along with the hustlers and working girls who made it famous.

These were also the years recognized as the birth of the modern sex workers' rights movement. In 1973, the American activist Margo St. James launched the first prostitutes' rights organization, Call Off Your Old Tired Ethics (COYOTE), to oppose the criminalization of prostitution; in 1975, more than one hundred prostitutes occupied a church in Lyon, France, to protest police repression, issuing statements that they would stay until prison sentences against their members were lifted. The movement for what was then called prostitutes' rights may have been born from demands for sexual freedom, but its own demands were for freedom from police violence.

It was these groups that laid the foundation for Carol Leigh's invention of the phrase sex worker, and through their networks of activists and allied organizations that "sex work" advanced. In the first decade of this century, United Nations Secretary-General Ban Ki-moon and several bodies within the UN called for an end to the criminalization of sex work; these included the Global Commission on HIV and the Law, which was created by the United Nations Development Program for the Joint UN Program on HIV/AIDS, an independent commission. The International Labor Organization recognizes sex work as labor and discrimination against sex workers—including forced HIV testing—as a violation of their labor rights. Human Rights Watch recommends the decriminalization of sex work. The World Health Organization recommends that "all countries should work toward decriminalization of sex work and elimination of the unjust application of non-criminal laws and regulations against sex workers."

All this isn't to say that with increased visibility sex workers' lives have unilaterally improved, that these recommendations have been adopted without struggle (if they have been adopted at all), or that a new focus on sex work as work has meant an end to the social phenomenon of prostitution.

In the not-quite-forty years that have passed since the invention of sex work, the public's fascination has only found new avenues for fulfillment, even as people involved in the sex trade have taken charge of their own depiction. Just as sex workers have taken up more public space in which to work and speak, each opportunity stands in contrast to the imaginary roles they are cast in. Prostitutes are still, for many people, just what's at the other end of the peep hole—or the handcuffs. As Anne McClintock observed in her 1992 essay "Screwing the System," "The more prostitutes are obliged to speak of their actions in public, the more they incriminate themselves." A prostitution arrest doesn't require actual sex (not that this stops police from pursuing sex themselves), but rather, only communications for the purpose of committing prostitution. If sex workers' speech is where whole lives are made criminal, how does that carry through to public demands to make sex workers' lives visible and relatable through "sharing our stories"?

McClintock argues, with reference not only to specific treatment in the courts but throughout sex workers' lives, that this is precisely the point of soliciting their testimonies: "By ordering the unspeakable to be spoken in public, . . . by obsessively displaying dirty pictures, filmed evidence, confessions, and exhibits, the prostitution trial reveals itself as structured around the very fetishism it sets itself to isolate and punish." Sex workers are to understand that they're outsiders and outlaws for selling their bodies, and yet what's called for in relaying their stories is the repetition of that sale, and to a much broader public than they encounter in their work.

Sex workers are called to give testimony on the nature of their work and lives in ever more venues: in secret diaries; on cable specials, opposite the "disgraced" politicians who hire them; to social workers, psychotherapists, and other members of the helping classes; and inside tabloids if they—or the ginned-up scandals created around them—have made headlines. Very rarely does sharing anything in these venues serve them, or the public. Sex workers are there for the sake of some unseen owners' profits.

These demands on their speech, to both convey their guilt and prove their innocence, are why, at the same time that sex work has made strides toward recognition and popular representations that defy stereotypes, prostitutes, both real and imagined, still remain the object of social control. This is how sex workers are still understood: as curiosities, maybe, but as the legitimate target of law enforcement crackdowns and charitable concerns—at times simultaneously. And so this is where the prostitute is still most likely to be found today, where those who seek to "rescue" her locate her: at the moment of her arrest.

3
The Work

"The prostitute" is stretched thin across the threshold of the literal and the metaphoric, put to work as almost no other figure is.

—Julia Bryan-Wilson, art historian (2012)

The first women who shared anything with me about prostitution were later arrested.

"Were you scared when you started?" I had asked. She stood at my kitchen counter buttering bread. We sat together at the table under the stairs that had once led to the servants' quarters, but now just led up to my room. I didn't know if I should be asking. Was it okay to ask? Did she want to tell me? And should she tell me? Would she think I thought I was too good to do what she did? Did my asking, my not knowing, the fact that I had to ask mean I didn't have it in me? Was I just like one of her customers, asking terrible questions, wasting her time?

She was patient with me. She had no reason to be.

The men, she said, would call the mobile phone number listed in an ad in the paper. Some met her in a motel or hotel but many also invited her into their homes, and in those homes they would leave their mail out, their family photos. It was astounding, she said, how many men felt so safe, to do that; that men maybe always feel safe, even around strangers who are women; that what she knew about these men's lives could put her in far more danger than if these men were cops.

How few people did she think she could tell any of this to? How many times was I, asking my own questions, just seeking a kind of validation? We are told that women, either by nature or otherwise, would never want or need to hear from someone that they think could be a whore. Would I be believable to customers, the ones I was just learning enough about to construct my own suspect values of: who those men were, and who I would be to them if we met. Could I be good enough for sex work?

I asked her, What did she do in her hour with them? How did she get from the phone call to the money to the act and then home again? Why was this path not immediately understandable to me when I had performed it time and again without the appearance of money? It was only because it had been made obscure to me, like so many feminine mysteries of sex that are actually maintained by men who prefer us ignorant and dependent.

A division had been constructed between them and me, prostitutes and all other women, which had resulted in a break in transmitting such vital information. It was the breakdown, not the sex work, that kept us apart, that could cause us to suffer unnecessarily. Now I wanted everyone to know exactly what it could be like, what their choices were, what power they had, should they ever be in the situation of explicitly trading sex for something they need.

I remembered the workshops during college, held each spring in a barn on a nearby campus where you could learn how to perform a menstrual extraction—which can be used as a form of abortion—at home. There was no subtext: This information was shared in case abortion was criminalized again in the United States. Did you ever want to have to use it? Most likely you didn't. Were you ashamed to know it? You should not be.

Recently I got an e-mail asking if I had any information on how to become a prostitute. The writer said that although she liked my work, it was not appropriate as a "101" resource on how to do sex work. That's true, but that doesn't mean that people reading it would not try to find advice in it anyway. It's what I did whenever I came across a book about prostitution or stripping, some years before I ever did sex work, reverse engineering the text into a how-to. This was before many people began to use the Internet to share this kind of information, certainly before sex workers kept blogs (though not quite before they started e-mail lists and discussions on Usenet).

Sex workers' ability to share information among themselves is essential for supporting all sex workers in negotiating their work, and in turning down work that is unsafe, underpaid, or undesirable. This is true of any job. But what does make this aspect of our work unique, and what creates the thump of panic in my gut when I open such an e-mail, is that to share this lifeline of information could be construed as criminal. Selling sex in the United States is a misdemeanor, but sharing information with someone about how to do it is considered a more serious criminal offense.

For sex workers, sharing honest information even anonymously means taking social, political, and emotional risks. Even in more uniformly legal forms of sex work—which in the United States could include pornography and stripping—secrecy reinforces stigma and shame and can compromise sex workers' ability to take control of their own labor. When sex workers are spoken of as having "double lives," rather than simply concealing who they are, this narrative obscures *why* it might be necessary for sex workers to conceal what they do at work. All that is intentionally discreet about sex work (protocols to ensure customer and worker privacy, for example) are strategies for managing legal risk and social exclusion and shouldn't be understood as deceptive any more than the discretion and boundaries a therapist or priest may maintain. But this necessary discretion warps under the weight of anti–sex work stigmas and policing; workers aren't sure what they can say and to who and not face consequences which themselves are unknown.

Remember Deborah Jeanne Palfrey, the famed "DC Madam" who, in the first decade of this century, counted David Vitter, the "family values" Republican senator from Louisiana, and the pro-abstinence soon-to-be-former AIDS czar Randall Tobias among her escort agency's clients? When she was charged with money-laundering and racketeering, her finances were seized, and her most marketable asset was her client list. In spring 2007, I found a page of it online, a phone bill with a typed list of numbers and corresponding towns, and the only unredacted phone number on it was the one at the bottom of the page—her own. Without her business, that client list was her last asset worth anything.

So I called her. I didn't take notes, but if I recall correctly she was looking to sell the list to a media outlet that would sift through it and track down the most high-profile customers. I may have made a soft bid for it: I had just launched a blog with the cofounder of the Sex Workers Outreach Project– USA, Stacey Swimme, and we were following Deborah Jeanne's case obsessively. ABC ended up with the list and put on a nighttime special program hyping it, only to declare they hadn't found anyone of significance on it. (Here's another name: Harlan Ullman, the man regarded as the architect of the shock-and-awe doctrine used by the Bush administration in the 2003 invasion of Iraq.) It did not stop the show, with its promise of "true tales" of prostitution. ABC was even calling us, asking if we could produce a "classy," "educated" (read: white, conventionally attractive) escort— like the ones they said Deborah Jeanne preferred to hire. Stacey and I took turns returning the bookers' calls, one of us playing the blogger and the other playing the escort, when in truth we were each both, and we compared notes on how much of the story's angle and progress the booker shared. To the blogger, he framed the story as an opportunity to show the "real world" of escorting, to present escorts without further objectifying them. In his phone call to the escort, he asked how soon they could meet for a preinterview at Starbucks. We declined his offers and kept going with the blog, where we could report the story instead of playing it.

There was something else about Deborah Jeanne's agency that captured our attention as much as it animated fantasies in the press: Reportedly, she required her workers to sign contracts stating that they wouldn't have sex with their customers. It's not an uncommon practice with agencies that offer outcall services, for which an escort, masseuse, or dancer travels to the customer's location. It's a legal fig leaf, an attempt to absolve the agency owners of liability and shunt it off onto the workers. But maintaining that fiction—however justifiable or necessary when prostitution is criminalized—also shuts down real-world talk about the actual content of these jobs. If you're not, as far as the paper says, having sex, why would the management ever need to acknowledge that negotiation about it is also part of the job? How can they address their workers' health and safety, like their need for condoms or lube? How can bosses provide legal support to their workers in the case of a sting when, to protect themselves, they insist the work is entirely legal?

It's not sex work but this kind of fiction and the criminal context that demands it that produces risks and hazards. Only in 2012 did a couple of US cities—San Francisco and Washington, DC—stop using condoms as evidence of prostitution, and did so only after considerable pressure from sex workers and public health and human rights advocates. In New York, the practice of using condoms as evidence of prostitution is so routine that the supporting depositions filled out by cops upon arrest have a standard field available to record the number of condoms seized from suspected sex workers. This is the tragedy of enforcement: A system that is supposed to use surveillance by law enforcement as a tool for combating violence against women (as prostitution is understood to be) produces violence against other, less defensible women. Sex workers refuse condoms from outreach workers, and from each other, as a way to stay safe from arrest.

These risks, not poor self-regard, are why sex workers might not share their experiences, even with each other.

There are other risks, too. So often in telling sex work stories, the storytelling process is a form of striptease indistinguishable from sex work itself, a demand to create a satisfyingly revealing story, for audiences whose interest is disguised as compassion or curiosity. In the conventional striptease routine, the sex worker dances suggestively for a first song, removes her top by the end of her second song and her bottom during the third. Off that stage, she knows there is also a script for how her story will be received. She's often accused of not being capable of sharing the truth of her own life, of needing translators, interpreters. But part of telling the truth here is refusing to conform the story to narrow roles—virgin, victim, wretch, or whore—that she did not herself originate.

The public is most accustomed to relating to sex workers through their sexuality—or more accurately, through a sexual performance that may or may not follow their sexuality off the job. The public may not perceive this as a performance, or alternatively, they may dismiss and fetishize it as fake. Whether they're received as brave truth tellers or conniving liars, the viewing public expects that this will be an erotic relationship whether or not they identify it as an erotic turn-on. Accordingly, sex workers calibrate what they share in public in order to compensate for this uncompensated erotic exchange.

This is not a peep show. So I will not, for example, be telling my story, though the means by which I came to the story I am telling here is inseparable from my experience as a sex worker. My job here is to reveal through an exchange of ideas, not through the incitement of arousal—while also not entirely putting aside that I have skin in this game.

Maintaining this kind of selective silence about myself is only a temporary, and ultimately insufficient, means of resistance. It's a tactic until the time comes, or is made to come, when I can share my story in legal and economic conditions more favorable to me and to others who still do sex work. While we wait, and also because it's just as important, I want to shift your gaze from sex workers to the fantasies of prostitution that occupy and obsess those who seek to abolish, control, or profit from sex work.

As a result of my political choice to remain silent on some of the questions we are taught to ask of sex workers, I worry that there might be so much absence in this story that it borders on erasure, that not speaking to those questions may cause some readers to think that there is almost no story here at all. Putting that privileged interrogation aside, however, will reveal all the space that is taken up by the idea of who the whore is. Rather than fear what we may be missing, I'll continue there.

4
The Debate

The sex work debate, no matter how sedate and sympathetic its interlocutors claim it to be, is a spectacle. It attracts an audience with the lure of a crisis—*prostitution sweeping the nation!*—and a promise of doing good by feeling terrible. Sad stories about sex work are offered like sequins, displayed to be admired and then swept off the stage when the number is done. As a treat, the organizers may even decide to invite a token whore to perform.

Here come the questions for her:

- Is prostitution violence against women?
- Are prostitutes "exploited" or are they "empowered"?
- What are the factors that lead women (and it's always women, and most often not trans women) to enter into or be forced to enter into prostitution?
- What about "the men" / "the johns" / "the demand side"?
- How can we help women "escape" / "exit from" / "leave" prostitution?
- How can we "raise awareness" about "this issue"?

Then there are the questions rarely up for debate, the ones she is left to raise alone:

- How do we define "prostitution"?
- How do people who sell sex describe it?
- What are some of the factors that lead women to *not* sell sex?
- What are some of the factors that lead women to oppose prostitution?
- How can we help women (and anyone else) better understand what selling sex is really like?
- How can we ensure that sex workers are leading any public debates on "this issue"—that is, about their own lives?

We should, in fact, refuse to debate. Sex work itself and, inseparable from it, the lives of sex workers are not up for debate—or they shouldn't be. I don't imagine that those in the antiprostitution camp who favor these kinds of debates actually believe that they are weighing the humanity, the value of the people who do sex work. (This assumes, of course, that there is a coherent antiprostitution camp, but for the sake of argument, let's limit it to the antiprostitution feminists and their allies loosely congregated in the secular left.) Their production of the debate rests on the assumption that they themselves comprise the group that really cares for prostitutes. They may consider the purpose of the prostitution debate to be the challenging of myths and assumptions, to demonstrate their own expertise, perhaps to "raise awareness."

What constitutes the nature of this awareness, particularly concerning the enduring and ubiquitous nature of prostitution, pornography, and other kinds of commercial sex? Awareness raisers can still count on a social hunger for lurid and detailed accounts, as well as a social order that restricts sex workers' own opportunities to speak out about the realities of their lives. These factors in combination promote demand for the debaters' own productions.

To fuel and stoke it, awareness raisers erect billboards on the sides of highways, with black-and-white photos of girls looking fearful and red letters crying NOT FOR SALE. They hire Hollywood bros like Ashton Kutcher and Sean Penn to make clicky little public service announcements for YouTube in which they tell their fans, "Real men don't buy girls." They occupy column inches in the *New York Times* with those such as Nicholas Kristof, who regales his readers with stories of his heroic missions into brothels and slums in Cambodia and in India "rescuing" sex workers.

The rescue industry, as anthropologist Laura Agustín terms such efforts, derives value from the production of awareness: It gives the producers jobs, the effectiveness of which is measured by a subjective accounting of how much they are being talked about. Raising awareness serves to build value for the raisers, not for those who are the subjects of the awareness.

Awareness raising about prostitution is not a value-neutral activity. Sex workers see a straight line between foundation dollars earmarked for advertisements such as those that appeared on Chicago buses—GET RICH. WORK IN

PROSTITUTION. PIMPS KEEP THE PROFITS, AND PROSTITUTED
WOMEN OFTEN PAY WITH THEIR LIVES.——and the allocation of
resources to the Chicago police to arrest pimps in order to
save women who they call "prostituted." Inevitably, all of
these women face arrest, no matter what they call them, a
demonstration of the harm produced by awareness raising
despite any good intentions. "On paper, sex workers are still
not as likely to face felony charges as their patrons," according to the *Chicago Reporter*, "who can be charged with a
felony on their first offense under the Illinois Safe Children's
Act, which was enacted in 2010." But when the paper exam-
ined felony arrest statistics they found,

> [the] data shows that prostitution-related felonies are being
> levied almost exclusively against sex workers. During the
> past four years, they made up 97 percent of the 1,266 prosti-
> tution-related felony convictions in Cook County. And the
> number only grew: Felony convictions among sex workers
> increased by 68 percent between 2008 and 2011.

This was when antiprostitution groups such as the Chicago
Alliance Against Sexual Exploitation became active in the
city, demanding johns pay.

With awareness raising as a goal, the debate circles back on
itself. The problem at hand is not, How do we improve the
lives of sex workers?, but, How should we continue to think
and talk about the lives of sex workers, to carry on our discourse
on prostitution regardless of how little sex workers are involved
in it? Perhaps those fixated on debating ought to confine the

scope of their solution to how to best bring about debates and leave those involved in the sex trade to themselves.

And on which side of this debate are sex workers presumed to sit?

Sex workers should not be expected to defend the existence of sex work in order to have the right to do it free from harm. For many, if not the majority, of people who work for a living, our attitudes toward our work change over the course of our working lives, even over the course of each day on the job. The experiences of sex workers cannot be captured by corralling them onto either the exploited or the empowered side of the stage. Likewise there must be room for them to identify, publicly and collectively, what they wish to change about how they are treated as workers without being told that the only solution is for them to exit the industry. Their complaints about sex work shouldn't be construed, as they often are, as evidence of sex workers' desire to exit sex work. These complaints are common to all workers and shouldn't be exceptional when they are made about sex work. As labor journalist Sarah Jaffe said of the struggles at her former job as a waitress, "No one ever wanted to save me from the restaurant industry."

The contemporary prostitution debate might appear to have moved on from the kinds of concerns moral reformers in the late nineteenth and early twentieth centuries expressed, but it has only slightly restated the question from, What do we do about prostitution? to, What do we do about prostitutes? According to the twenty-first-century heirs to the battle for moral hygiene, this is to be understood as a way of focusing on the prostitute as victim, not criminal. Forgive sex workers if they do not want the attention of those who refuse to listen to them.

Far from concerning the lives of people who do sex work, these debates are an opportunity for prostitution opponents to stake out their own intellectual, political, and moral contributions to "this issue." When feminist prostitute and COYOTE founder Margo St. James sought to debate antiprostitution activist Kathleen Barry at one of the first world conferences on trafficking in 1983, she was told by Barry that it would be "inappropriate to discuss sexual slavery with prostitute women." This continues to this day, with antiprostitution groups alleging that sex workers who want to participate in the same forums they do are "not representative," are members of a "sex industry lobby," or are working on behalf of—or are themselves—"pimps and traffickers." For my reporting on anti–sex work campaigners, I've been told I must be getting published only because I've been paid off by pimps. (So pimps are stealing wages from sex workers in order to give them to journalists?)

Barry went on to found the Coalition Against Trafficking in Women, which introduced the vague of sense "sexual exploitation" into United Nations and United States anti-trafficking policy, used by some to mean all commercial sex, whether or not force, fraud, or coercion are present. Sweden's famed prostitution law, often described as a feminist victory for criminalizing men who by sex, and which Barry and her anti–sex work allies in Equality Now and the European Women's Lobby push as model legislation, was undertaken without any meaninful consultation with women who sell sex. By contrast, New Zealand's model of decriminalized prostitution was advanced by sex workers, and has since been evaluated with their participation (and largely to their satisfaction). Rather than evolving toward more sex worker involvement in policy, however, the backlash is nearly constant. Canada's Supreme Court agreed to hear a case that could result in removing laws against prostitution, and now in appeals, the same body declined to hear testimony from advocacy organizations run by sex workers themselves.

We must redraw the lines of the prostitution debate. Either prostitutes are in the debate or they are not. Sex workers are tired of being invited to publicly investigate the politics of their own lives only if they're also willing to serve as a prop for someone else's politics. As editor of the influential anthology *Whores and Other Feminists* Jill Nagle writes, "one could argue that the production of feminist discourse around prostitution by non-prostitutes alienates the laborer herself from the process of her own representation." Not only are sex workers in the abstract used to aid feminists in "giving voice to the voiceless," those same feminists then remain free to ignore the content of sex workers' actual speech.

When sex workers are cast in this role, as mute icon or service instrument, it's the antiprostitution camp at work, decrying sex workers' situation yet abandoning them to the fundamentally passive role they insist sex workers occupy in prostitution. The parallel becomes even more damning when sex workers are paid comparatively little for their participation behind the debate podiums.

The Demand for "Demand"

The story about prostitution that occasions and results from these so-called debates is one of moral contagion and elite panic: Sex work is everywhere, it's growing, it's out of control, it makes many billions of dollars a year. It's coming for your daughter, and it's in your backyard, and if it hasn't and it's not yet, it will be. FROM INSTANT MESSAGE TO INSTANT NIGHTMARE! warn ads out of the Florida attorney general's office; a young girl cowers under the red slash of the headline.

In all the ways that narratives about commercial sex once mirrored fears about the unruly, uncivilized, unhealthy, unfeminist women who perform it, now they more closely resemble fears of the demand for commercial sex. The fears focus on the same thing: desire and sex workers' bodies; they presumably have been relieved from being made targets by being remade into victims requiring expert intervention. "The endless supply of victims won't cease," states former US ambassador Swanee Hunt's antiprostitution group, Demand Abolition, "until we combat the driver of sex trafficking: demand for illegal commercial sex."

The demand for victims, as anti–sex work activists describe it, is driven by men's insatiable desire—not by sex workers' own demands for housing, health care, education, a better life, a richer life, if we dare. Male desire is held up as a problem to be solved, and ending men's "demand" for "buying" women is a social project to be taken up by producing alternatives for men—such as jail—and scant alternatives for sex workers—such as other forms of employment. It's a smaller and more convenient problem to want to solve: who men want to fuck and how. It's one that women who oppose sex work and sex workers' rights can pretend—unlike poverty or racial inequality—that they have no role in, that they do not themselves benefit from.

Male desire isn't the only source of panic. It's also how men use technology to, as antiprostitution advocates term it, buy and sell women. Today the Internet is cast as the vehicle for unchecked male desire to purchase sex, the same panic that was once stoked by the telephone, without which we could not have had the call girl, or by escort ads in the backs of alternative newspapers. New mediums have often been said to have a corrupting influence on the weak (women, usually).

In more subtle but no less instrumental ways, sex work in the new millennium has been aided by the expansion of the service and leisure industries, which offer, as just one example, enjoyment in the course of business travel in unfamiliar hotels and on solitary nights. All the reasons a hotel is bland and lonely to the traveler are the same reasons they'd want to populate it with more pleasant company, company that can be hired on demand. Pay-per-view pornography is widespread and uncontroversial (and a high percentage of overall porn profits, according to the industry's own account, are reaped by the Marriott, Hilton, and Westin corporations); free Wi-Fi is the next mandatory convenience, which, for the solo traveler on an expense account, will transmit porn and outcall sex work ads even more anonymously.

Commercial sex adapts to its social and economic surroundings, and all the while its practice also influences their shape: the saloon in the mining town; the dance hall for the working class and the assignation house for the wealthy; the private call girl's apartment in a nice enough neighborhood; the after-hours karaoke bar undetected by day; the 24/7 porn theater right off a mass transit stop; the abandoned pier that hums to life with cruisers and couples; the rural brothel far from home; the strip club along the turnpike.

We don't think of these places as red-light districts, those upper floors of business-class hotels that can be reached only by the swipe of a key card in the elevator, but these spaces are now much more likely to play host to commercial sex than any nearby street corner—if there even is still a street corner close to the great mall and tourist sprawl these hotels are set down in and make profitable.

The process of moving sex work into the private sphere can be mapped along broader trends toward sexual gentrification, as identified by author and longtime AIDS activist Sarah Schulman. This process began long before the popularization of the Internet and was as driven by rising rents as it was by public neglect in response to AIDS. "Gay life is now expected to take place in private," Schulman observed of historically gay neighborhoods in New York in her book *The Gentrification of the Mind*, "by people who are white, upper class, and sexually discreet." Law enforcement worked in tandem with gentrifiers to both produce and justify "street sweeps." New York City mayor Rudolph Giuliani didn't just need the New York Police Department to put down Times

Square; he also needed Disney to move in. And, to an extent, he needed Craigslist to finish it off.

Through zoning and through fear-fueled bias, sexually oriented businesses have been isolated from "legitimate" businesses—and yet, never completely. With its move into private spaces, they won't be for much longer. The gentrification of the red-light district and the migration of commercial sex to the Internet don't spell the end of the sex industry so long as actual live bodies must meet and exchange somewhere, and that somewhere has always been close to the places people live and work, all activities simultaneously happening behind closed doors. At the same time, all that was once negotiated on the street is now also conducted on public Web sites, and under more watchful (and curious) and tracking eyes than ever. Yet it is also possible for many people to try out sex work, organized online and conducted in private, without risking becoming a known prostitute. It's the kind of privacy that, as author and former call girl Tracy Quan commented in an interview with the blog *Tits and Sass*, is more valuable than ever in the information age. "Facebook didn't exist," she points out, "when twentieth-century prostitutes were developing their political rhetoric" of coming out and being out.

Is this the real fear then: not that more people are becoming prostitutes but that the conventional ways we'd distinguish a prostitute from a nonprostitute woman are no longer as functional? Antiprostitution laws are primarily about exclusion and banishment; how, now, will we know who is to banished and excluded? And from the perspective of a (potential) sex worker: If you no longer have to go to a particular and stigmatized place, if you don't have to already be part of a social network of other sex workers in order to get information about it, the social and material risks of doing sex work are more navigable. It's not, I think, that sex work has necessarily gotten much safer through its gentrification, but that, like chic coffee bars and restaurants moving into previously working-class neighborhoods, gentrified sex work brings along with it consumers and workers who might never before have ventured there. It's not clear whether the sex industry is expanding, but it's definitely changing in character.

Crisis or Convergence

As some forms of commercial sex have been decriminalized, and workplaces have formalized, we have begun dismantling the systems of control that put sex workers at risk. This transformation of the sex industry calls into question why these systems—laws prohibiting "loitering with intent to solicit," "living off the earnings," "keeping a bawdy house," for example—and those whose job it is to enforce them, and to "rehabilitate" those caught up in that enforcement, exist at all. The rationale in all these systems of control, whether they are meant to regulate or abolish commercial sex, is that they will make commercial sex unsavory enough to deter involvement. What were conceived of as systems of control are, in reality, systems of producing and doling out harmful consequences.

Some of those consequences are lessening, not through any learned or compassionate overhaul, but through sex workers' own labor of adapting to the conditions of gentrification and making sex work more private: developing Internet-based businesses and creating social networks independent of red-light districts in which to share information and tactics.

Sociologists Barbara Brents, Crystal Jackson, and Kathryn Hausbeck, in *The State of Sex*, describe this facet of the gentrification of the sex industry as a "convergence"—a blending of what is understood as the sex industry with the leisure and pleasure industries. Convergence describes two near-simultaneous movements. One is the growing dominance of service and leisure economies, along with a normalization of purchasing intimate services: child care, Brazilian waxes, personal training. The other is the formalizing of sexually oriented businesses: the corporate consolidation of strip club ownership, the proliferation of Internet porn business, the growth of independently operated escort services advertised online.

Even the practice of finding a sugar daddy has been brought to a global market through paid membership Web sites that resemble conventional dating sites, though the wink and nod is that the young women on these sites would not be dating these men if money were not changing hands. The wink is only a slight one; these sites can be found advertised alongside escort services in free tabloids, but their real publicity comes from mainstream news coverage in outlets like the *New York Times* or on CNN.

"As these businesses become more visible and main-stream," Brents, Jackson, and Hausbeck argue, "the business practices and work within them are becoming more routinized, and many look more and more like other service and leisure economies." That is, the industry formerly known as the sex industry is not, as antiprostitution social reformers have alleged, some creeping menace ever-present at the margins of society that must be confined and tamed through purifying legislative effort. The margins are shifting. The crisis was never one of morals, but of money.

5

The Industry

There is no one sex industry. Escorting, street hustling, hostessing, stripping, performing sex for videos and webcams—the range of labor makes speaking of just one feel inadequate. To collapse all commercial sex that way would result in something so flat and shallow that it would only reinforce the insistence that all sex for sale results from the same phenomenon—violence, deviance, or desperation.

This variety also extends to the regulation and policing of workplaces, all having varying degrees of formality and legality. Even those operating under the most intense criminalization, in the least understood sectors of what's come to be called the informal economy, have methods of organization and convention that are kept intentionally private, discreet, and contained within the industry. It would appear that even many scholars of the informal economy who've mapped the labor of trash pickers and street sellers, counterfeiters and smugglers have failed to give sex work its due—because it is criminal, because it is service work, and in many cases, because it is work gendered as female. They are confined to a "floating city," as sociologist Sudhir Venkatesh describes it in his book of the same name, somehow outside society. Journalist Robert Neuwirth, in *Stealth of Nations: The Global Rise of the Informal Economy*, seeks to delink underground work from criminality, yet not for sex workers, who are only present in metaphor.

I'll describe just one workplace that has been almost entirely overlooked: a commercial dungeon—which is in reality just a house on a residential block in a suburb of a major American city, connected by public transit to its central business district and those who work there. This is not a marginal place, nor is it a place marked by transgression. It's only called a dungeon so that clients seeking the services of those who work there can know what to expect—versus, say, a massage studio or a gentlemen's club. There is no one held in chains but those who pay to be placed in them, and even then, only for an agreed time.

In a dungeon a client can expect that several workers are available on each shift, and some workers will want to do what he wants to and some won't. A receptionist will take his call, or answer his e-mail, and assign him to a worker based on what he'd like, the worker's preferences, and mutual availability. Some dungeons might post their workers' specialties on a Web site. They might also keep them listed in a binder next to the phone, the workers each taking turns playing receptionist, matching clients to workers over their shift. After each appointment the worker would write up a short memo and file it for future reference should the client call again, so that others would know more about him.

The dungeon is informal only to the extent that the labor producing value inside its walls isn't regarded as real work. There are shift meetings, schedules, and a commission split based on seniority. Utility bills arrive, and are paid. Property taxes, too. In some cases the manager would give discreet employment references. And sometimes people were fired.

There was one group of people who did perform unwaged work in the dungeon: the many male "houseboys" who would telephone, at least once each day, to ask to come and clean. The women who worked in the dungeon knew that managing these men's slave fantasies was itself a form of work, but when they could just turn them loose on the dishes, the worst they would have to do is check later to see if anything untoward had happened to a glass or fork. It was never meant as a commentary on the years of feminists' arguing over the value of housework, but it still could feel deeply gratifying that the houseboys were made to understand their only reward would be the empty sink.

This—the notes, the bills, the dishes—is the look inside a dungeon you'll get when you work there, not when you're paying for it.

On an opposite coast, there was the college town escort agency "run" by R., who really was just the one who paid for the ad in the back of the paper each week and the mobile phone that customers would call after seeing the ad. The women who shared the ad and phone line paid R. a share of each half-hour or hour appointment they got through the ad, which meant they didn't need to be around all the time to pick up the phone or give any information about themselves to the newspaper that ran the ad. They just showed up at the motel room or house where they'd meet their customers. Every once in a while a woman would call the phone number, wanting to work with them, and R. would meet with them in a coffee shop. If they decided to work together, she'd train them on all of this. Some of the women took turns answering the phone and booking appointments, and after they learned how to manage that, they'd end up going off on their own.

And there was M., who modeled for a few "shemale" Web sites. This was not a term she used to describe herself, but she made most of her money escorting men who were fans of those sites to sex parties held in clubs and other semiprivate venues—whether or not they had sex, which they did sometimes. The Web sites were ways to advertise herself as a date for hire without having to pay to be featured in online escort ad directories, and when the customers would e-mail her as fans, they could make plans to meet up. M. would make it clear that she would be paid for their meeting as well. A friend of hers was busted when an undercover cop contacted her through an overt online escort ad, made an appointment, and then arrested her in her own apartment, also taking her phone and her laptop. M. wasn't as fearful of having an encounter with police at the club.

And there was C., who ran a porn site out of the apartment she shared with her boyfriend. In addition to modeling for her own porn, she also recruited others from the online forums she posted in, or through friends who knew what she did for a living. When a model came to C.'s apartment to shoot, the only contact she'd have with anyone associated with the porn site was C., who also acted as photographer. C.'s work computer was her personal computer; her workplace was her living room—a couch, a photo backdrop, her DVDs, and her cats. Sometimes she ran out of money to pay for models and would just shoot herself until more memberships came in. Sometimes fans would ask her to visit them in other cities and pay for her to fly out and shoot models there. The money could be unpredictable. She used to work in a strip club to supplement it.

Though these are four of the most visible forms of sex work—porn, stripping, domination, and escorting—and each offers a distinct environment, it's not uncommon for workers to draw their incomes from more than one. It's about more than maximizing their earning potential; it's also a way to negotiate the varying degrees of exposure and surveillance that come with each venue. For every escort who would never give up her privacy by working in a strip club, chancing that someone she knew would come in, there's a stripper who would never give up her privacy by working in porn or having her image posted online, and there's a porn performer who would never have sex for money outside the context of a porn shoot.

These are also only anecdotes drawn from sex workers I've met and worked with over the last ten years, in this first decade of the twenty-first century, and in the United States. Each involves some work online and offline. Each caters to customers in a specific way, and with its own conventions: Web sites sell photo sets and memberships; escort services set up appointments; clubs charge entrance fees and sell drinks;

and performers sell stage shows and private dances. Each sell takes its own skills, has its own hustle, its own downsides.

However, as distinct as the work and their environments may be, there is a political usefulness in calling all of this sex work, while also insisting that it varies considerably over time and place. The portrait of street-level prostitution, for example, as it's on display in media accounts—a woman, most often a woman of color, standing in a short skirt and leaning into a car or pacing toward one—is a powerful yet lazily constructed composite. As the lead character of the prostitute imaginary, she becomes a stand-in for all sex workers, a reduction of their work and lives to one fantasy of a body and its particular and limited performance for public consumption. Sex workers' bodies are rarely presented or understood as much more than interchangeable symbols— for urban decay, for misogyny, for exploitation—even when propped up so by those who claim some sympathy, who want to question stereotypes, who want to "help."

The character isn't even representative of all the street-soliciting sex workers she stands in for. When considering the practice of street-based sex work, sociologist Elizabeth Bernstein observes, "It is important to recognize the extent to which the practices and meanings of sexual labor varied in the different prostitution strolls," even in the same city. Some of this sex work can be more accurately described as trade or barter, Bernstein writes, "self-organized, occasional exchanges that generally took place within women's own homes and communities." She distinguishes this from "the sexual labor of 'career' streetwalkers," in which "commercial sexual exchange was conceptualized as 'work' that resided in the public display of the body." You find this echoed in the research of Chicago youth involved in the sex trade conducted by the grassroots group Young Women's Empowerment Project. They've adopted the descriptor "sex trades and street economies" to recognize that, for their community, trading sex for what they need to survive isn't necessarily understood as their "work," and that it occurs alongside other informal labor, such as hair braiding or babysitting.

The sex industry is varied and porous throughout. Consider its other most visible outpost in America: the legal brothels of rural Nevada in the few counties where prostitution was never fully criminalized, and where strict regulation and isolation are employed to make it tolerable to the public. There, according to a recent study conducted by Brents, Jackson, and Hausbeck and published in *The State of Sex*, one third of brothel workers had never done any other kind of sex work before, but rather came to it directly from "non-sexual service work." Three quarters of those they interviewed move between "straight work" and sex work. "Selling sex," they write, "is often one form of labor among a variety of jobs."

When we say that sex work is service work, we don't say that just to sanitize or elevate the status of sex workers, but also to make plain that the same workers are performing sex work and nonsexual service work. In her study of Rust Belt strippers published in *Policing Pleasure: Sex Work, Policy, and the State in Global Perspective*, Susan Dewey observed that the vast majority of the dancers—all but one—at one club in upstate New York had worked outside the sex industry, and "many had left intermittently for low-wage, service-sector work elsewhere before returning with the recognition that they preferred the topless bar with its possibility of periodic windfalls from customers." For the dancers who Dewey surveyed, it was the work *outside* of the sex industry that was "exploitative, exclusionary, and without hope for social mobility or financial stability."

Opponents, from the European Women's Lobby to reactionary feminist bloggers, like to claim that sex workers insist it is "a job like any other," but sex workers do not make this claim—unless by this anti–sex work activists agree with sex workers that the conditions under which sexual services are offered can be as unstable and undesirable as those cutting cuticles, giving colonics, or diapering someone else's babies.

But that's not what sex work opponents are referring to when they snap back with a phrase such as "a job like any other." When they say "jobs" they don't mean those informal service jobs, but their more elevated labor administering social projects, conducting research, and lobbying. Rescuing sex workers is good work for them. As feminist anarchist Emma Goldman noted in 1910, the prostitution panic "will help to create a few more fat political jobs—parasites who stalk about the world as inspectors, investigators, detectives, and so forth." The loss of sex workers' income was their gain.

Opponents even take our jobs when we win. Socialist feminist activist and antiracist campaigner Selma James, in her essay "Hookers in the House of the Lord," documents the closure of a successful grassroots sex workers' legal project in

London in the eighties, so "feminist lawyers and women from the anti-porn lobby" could create their own without having to actually employ the sex workers who started this advocacy. "What we are witnessing before our very eyes is the process whereby women's struggle is hidden from history and transformed into an industry," James writes, "jobs for the girls."

The message of anti–sex work feminists is, It's the women working against sex work who are the real hard workers, shattering glass ceilings and elevating womanhood, while the tramps loll about down below. As political theorist Kathi Weeks notes, to call a woman a tramp is to judge the value of a woman's sexuality *and* labor. Tramps, she writes in *The Problem with Work*, are "potentially dangerous figures that could, unless successfully othered, call into question the supposedly indisputable benefits of work"—and home and family, and women's commitment to all of it. When sex workers are "rescued" by anti–sex work reformers, they are being disciplined, set back into their right role as good women. This isn't just the province of large NGOs; one-woman rescue missions have popped up online and in megachurches, projects that claim to support themselves through the sale of candles and jewelry made by rescued sex workers. These jobs may technically exist outside the sex industry, but without a supply of rescued workers, there would be no cheap labor, no candles—and there would be no projects for the rescuers to direct.

These demands on sex workers' labor, while it is simultaneously devalued, is why we still insist that sex work is *work*. But this should not be confused with uncritical sentiment, as if sex work is only work if it's "good" work, if we love to do it. Being expected to perform affection for our jobs might feel familiar to sex workers—management at the unionized peep show the Lusty Lady tried to insert language in their contract that the job was meant to be "fun," which the dancers refused to accept. To insist that sex workers only deserve rights at work if they have fun, if they love it, if they feel empowered by it is exactly backward. It's a demand that ensures they never will.

6

The Peephole

Klute is Jane Fonda's star turn as a call girl, for which she won an Oscar, and all throughout it she's radiant—in a backless, silver-mirrored dress, in her shag, in a swingers' cocktail lounge. Before we are allowed to see her we are introduced to her voice, surreptitiously recorded by an unknown man. The recording, played first with the opening credits, is a one-sided solicitation. She assures us we are going to have a good time. We listen to her voice, and the tape loop spins; we're overhearing her private conversations with a customer. We might think we know something, but all that we learn is that the way to know a call girl is when she doesn't know we are listening. An alternative would require her participation, or her consent.

This is the way that we come to know a sex worker, not only in *Klute* but in other prostitute media, from *Memoirs of a*

Woman of Pleasure to the columns of Nicholas Kristof in the *New York Times*. We know her through the author's interpretation of the words and poses she chooses to represent herself with to her clientele. The novelist's and reporter's and researcher's eyes graze over whatever window, physical or digital, in which she leans. Aside from an origin story of her life "before," this is where the exposition will be confined: the red light, the bed, the men, the money. Everything else is out of frame. This is her everything—until she turns her back on it.

It's how *Klute* introduces us to this style of reportage, however limited, that we should receive it: as a single moment in one woman's life, captured on tape, and stuck on repeat.

Surveillance is a way of knowing sex workers that unites the opportunity for voyeurism with the monitoring and data collection performed by law enforcement, by social service providers, or by researchers. Even under surveillance, sex workers' own words aren't to be trusted without the mediation of those who are almost always regarded as superior outside experts. As motivation, such surveillance isn't meant to expand the public knowledge of the lives of sex workers; it's to investigate some form of harm to the public that's believed to originate with them.

AIDS occasioned one such investigation, but not before sex workers were scapegoated as "vectors of disease" who—it was claimed, with misunderstood evidence—would endanger the public; that is, the families of men who paid for sex. "'The Prostitute Study,'" writes historian Melinda Chateauvert in *Sex Workers Unite*, "didn't require participants to be sex workers, and most of the 180 women who volunteered for it had never done sex work." The 1986 study didn't attempt to trace transmission but rather the prevalence of the virus in women. It took on a life of its own in the press and public imagination, she adds, and "when male AIDS researchers heard about the study to track the virus in women, they assumed the subjects were prostitutes." This and an earlier Walter Reed study of ten soldiers who reported that they contracted HIV after sexual contact with "prostitutes" was mischaracterized as evidence that women—still assumed to be prostitutes—could transmit HIV to men through straight sex. "To Walter Reed doctors, it was obvious that prostitutes were disease vectors," writes Chateauvert. "They were wrong, but the idea stuck."

As we have moved from the panic of the period of AIDS crisis to what Sarah Schulman calls the era of "Ongoing AIDS," the new site of sex work panic is the Internet. New technologies, we are told by the press and politicians, have made new forms of sexual commerce available as never before in history. And as the technological innovations supporting sex work have expanded, they are used to justify new forms of surveillance.

Invisible Women

The prostitute is imagined as an invisible woman, a voiceless woman, a woman concealed even in public, in her nudity—in all her presumed availability. I say "is imagined," but there are many people who take part in this imagining, who are invested in it. I remember paging through a phone book as a kid, flipping to the "E" section and finding the ads for escorts. No actual women were pictured, nothing explicit. Escorts were revealed with clip art: a woman in a long gown that hung off one shoulder, a white woman with shoulder-length hair, her fingers to her lips. There may have been a moon drawn in the background. There were lipstick prints, another popular graphic element of the time. It was the eighties, and this was the palette the phone book designers had to draw on: No one created clip art just for escorts, so all the images that could signify women or glamour or class were strung together. A careful reader of the lipstick and the bare shoulders against the curls of text, words such as "elite," "private," "upscale," and the perennial "discreet," could interpret them. They could imagine whatever they want.

Even in full-color ads reproduced nearly infinitely across the Web, the sex worker herself may not be present. There are good reasons: not wanting to be outed and not trusting the publishers to protect the records linking the payment information—legal identification, a credit card—with the purchaser. As a result, escort and outcall dancers' agencies may run stock photos of women who have never even worked for them, and independent escorts and models might select photos that show only specific body parts, particularly as they may relate to their marketing niches: long hair, small breasts, a round ass, toned legs. Some sex workers, particularly those who do it only occasionally, may want to leave their ads on the Internet for only the periods that they are actually working. For the most part, sex workers want to minimize their exposure and preserve their privacy while also earning a living.

When I first saw online sex work ads, I couldn't believe that the police would allow them to exist. They appeared in many forms: expensively lit glamour photos arranged in slide shows, by outfit or fantasy theme; casual motel-room mirror self-portraits with a few hasty lines of text, a phone number, and clear instructions not to call from a blocked line; elaborate portfolio Web sites listing favorite books, shoes, and dietary restrictions; vague solicitations that had a single, striking photo and an e-mail address.

But of course the cops have an interest in these ads, if not in their creative flourishes: Online ads provide a steady flow of people to target in their vice operations: to monitor sex workers' activities and set them up for stings. They allow cops to build databases of their working names, photos, mobile phone numbers, locations, services offered, prices, and availability. In some cases police have impersonated customers in order to gain access to sex workers' private online forums, including databases of dangerous clients. A typical vice patrol still doesn't make this many sex workers immediately available to police for such systematic surveillance.

And yet for sex workers the trade-offs of online advertising still make all these risks worth taking. We know about the games of cat and mouse with the police that are used to chase working girls from apartment to apartment, corner to corner. Once Craigslist, the world's largest free classified-ad Web site, became a target, sex workers moved to Backpage, a classified ads site owned by Village Voice

Media, once the publishers of the venerable alternative newspaper the *Village Voice*. Then the same coalitions of cops, conservatives, and anti–sex work feminists that railed against Craigslist moved on to Backpage, too. At this rate they can just follow sex workers around until there's no Internet left to advertise on. But really, their aim is to wear down any publisher who might consider hosting sex workers' ads, and to raise the costs of doing business for anyone involved in the trade.

"How Pimps Use the Web to Sell Girls" headlines one of *New York Times* columnist Nicholas Kristof's anti-Backpage columns, which number in the dozens. An Equality Now petition demands that the "*Village Voice* must end its complicity in the rape and exploitation of girls and women." Craigslist was called "the Walmart of sex trafficking" by antiprostitution campaigners so often that it became hard to trace who started it, let alone on what basis they could make that claim.

It is terrible, they claim, that anyone is "being sold." This is how they describe these ads, as if a sellers and buyers use them to exchange human beings. They cannot fathom that the person in the ad could be the seller herself, so they fix their anguish on the publisher, as if the "products" and the markets in which the advertisements are bought and sold are the same. In the absence of a pimp or a trafficker to blame, they target the publisher. The solution offered? Renounce these ads, which, now that publishing an ad has been made synonymous with selling a person, will stand in for actually doing anything practical or beneficial for those people in the ads.

The choice to target the ads reveals what anti–sex work campaigners believe about the industry and its impact on sex workers' lives. The near pornographic focus proves what campaigners view as the real threat: the visibility of sex work. Their anguish over advertisements has less to do with concern for how the people in them might be treated in the course of their work and much more to do with expressing their own negative feelings about sex work. We can't bear imagining the horrors we assume untold behind these ads, say the anti–sex work reformers, and we will solve this by ensuring that no one can place them.

Through such demands, reformers take away from sex workers the power to make these decisions about their own labor. Where the Internet has opened up opportunities for them to take control of their work by increasing their direct access to customers, it has also given law enforcement, politicians, and assorted anti–sex work types a highly visible and vulnerable place to attack. They claim they're "protecting" sex workers when they demand that publishers refuse their ads. But for the workers themselves, losing ad venues means losing control over how they negotiate at work.

This strategy, so far, is working. In December 2012, the *Village Voice* announced that anyone wishing to place an adult ad in their paper would be limited to using "face shots," or photographs clearly showing the sex worker's face. "Flesh. We are not against it at the *Village Voice*. Actually, we think it's one of the best parts of being alive. But you'll find less of it in this issue. That's no accident," their new publisher announced in a statement that must not have been vetted by any office feminists (or even Google) titled "Our Bodies, Ourselves." It's damning enough that the *Voice* caved to people opposed to the existence of sex work. But to require any sex worker who wants to place an ad to show her face? The editor's note continues:

> Many of us here at the *Voice* wish these ads would just go away. And, in fact, they continue to migrate online, so that might happen soon enough. There is not much doubt that the new rules are going to make us less appealing to this kind of customer. That is a price we are willing to pay.

What a price, one which the *Voice* can shift, along with the opprobrium and legal threats, back to sex workers. "Our bodies" indeed.

Where this strategy is not yielding such easy returns for the campaigners is when their challenges actually make it through the courts. The few laws they've gotten passed that target online venues for sex workers' ads have met successful challenges not only from Backpage but from the Internet Archive, who were represented by the Electronic Frontier Foundation. In Washington State, a judge found a law against sex work ads was written so broadly that it would infringe on all online speech. In Tennessee, a judge declared that even an attempt to focus on "sex trafficking" in ads would possibly open grounds to attack all sex workers' ads, that "the state may not use a butcher knife on a problem that requires a scalpel to fix."

While the campaigners blame sites such as Craigslist and

Backpage both for the growth of the trade and for any harms related to it, they do so *for* sex workers, not *with* them. The campaigns make use of their images as evidence, but sex workers themselves are ignored. The prostitute is imagined by these self-identified defenders of her dignity; she can't speak for herself. She requires many interpreters. Not only have antiprostitution feminists attempted to shut down sex workers' ads, they've also manipulated them into data points to support their actions. An Atlanta-based organization with the imaginatively patronizing name A Future, Not A Past (AFNAP) hired a market research firm to conduct a study of prostitution on Craigslist. "Researchers" working for the firm, The Schapiro Group, who had never before researched prostitution, trawled through the ads, scrutinized the photos and text, and based only on this content guessed at the age of each person depicted. Never mind that Craigslist ads can be posted multiple times each day, or that each doesn't necessarily correlate to one individual—or any real individual. Dummy and repeat ads are part of the business. This either eluded or just didn't concern AFNAP, which advertised their findings along with a lavishly produced "tool kit" adorned with a photo of a young woman, her face downcast, covered in a hoodie, captioned "stop the prostitution of our nation's children."

Based on this amateurish tally of Craigslist, as well as surveillance of "street activity" and "hotels," AFNAP claimed that "as many as 200 to 300 young girls are commercially sexually exploited every month in Georgia," including "approximately 100 to 115 girls [who] are made available

through Craigslist.org ads each month, with profitable results," as they reported to the Georgia state legislature
in order to rally for tougher anti-prostitution legislation in
their state. Their "methodology" was repeated in similar
studies in Minnesota, Michigan, and New York, supported by
the Women's Funding Network, whose director Deborah
Richardson used such numbers to claim before a subcommit-
tee of the House Judiciary investigating Craigslist that "over
the past six months, the number of underage girls trafficked
online has risen exponentially in three diverse states." She did
not mention that this "exponential" increase were measured
based on counts of how many men had answered fake escort
ads created by Schapiro Group researchers, using photos of
young-looking women, and not from actual reported cases of
underage girls being trafficked. Such well-intentioned red-
light wandering has the sheen of science, even as it pays for
weeks of researchers' time scrolling through ads, just like
clients do.

Red-Light Neighbors

A better and offline equivalent to model our red-light wandering on might be the insider account of Samuel R. Delany,
whose participant observation of Times Square in its last pre-
Disney gasps is as much of the porn theaters as it is about
them and what they meant to those who cared for them.
Times Square Red, Times Square Blue maps the various forms
and sites of labor—theaters, food carts, camera shops, shoe-
shine stands, hustlers—and the kinds of people who frequent

each, including himself, and his unguarded affection for the porn theaters and the anonymous sexual encounters they made possible. For Delany, the value in a red-light district like the one once bounded by the streets around West Forty-Second Street and Eighth Avenue isn't just sexual pleasure, though it's that, too. The red-light district signals the potential of contact—physical, mental, spiritual—that crosses class.

I've worked in just one red-light district—San Francisco's North Beach, which is dotted still with strip clubs and porn shops, all crowned by the legendary City Lights Bookstore, which published and defended Allen Ginsberg's *Howl*, on the southwestern edge, and by Caffe Trieste, which has opera on its jukebox and old men with nothing to do but read the paper all day, up the hill to the northeast. In the streets sloping in between—Broadway, Kearny, Stockton—tourists cram together and drift between novelty Italian restaurants draped in garlic and roses and dumpling shops with whole chickens hanging in the windows. The purple neon marks the sex businesses, side by side with youth hostels, bars, corner stores, and cafes. We were all neighbors.

Forget the particulars of the work performed inside The Hungry I or the Lusty Lady or the Garden of Eden and appreciate the conditions of our shared neighborhood. You could take a public bus to and from a shift, step out on a break for a croissant at Happy Donut or a slice at Golden Boy, buy a magazine or a razor at the corner store on the way home. You had, all throughout your workday or night, the opportunity for human contact outside your workplace itself. It wasn't necessary to drive out to the industrial zone on the edge of town, you had other plausible reasons to be in the neighborhood, you were both anonymous and safe in the way you are in a city. You were, like everyone else who belonged to the neighborhood, another set of eyes on the street.

When Craigslist's Erotic Services section launched, it wasn't the first Web site where sex workers could place ads seeking customers, but it was the first to so closely resemble the geography of the red-light districts that preceded it. Remember that Times Square didn't contain only sexually-oriented businesses; as Delany captured it, the neighborhood was home to a variety: to low-end electronics and jewelry shops; to single-room occupancy hotels; to street-level workers informally selling sex; to those selling kebabs and newspapers. As threatening as it might be that a site such as Craigslist provided a space for advertising sexual commerce, what's perhaps more threatening is that it did so alongside advertisements for any other kind of product or service imaginable. Rather than segregate sexual commerce, Craigslist made sex workers neighbors.

But consider this first: All sexual commerce is technological. Before electricity provided automation, the first peep shows operated under manual candlelight. Before telephones, or even telegraphs, prostitutes carried printed business cards. In ancient Greece, certain classes of prostitutes attracted customers by scoring the words "Follow me" on the soles of their sandals, leaving a trail in the streets behind them. Prostitution itself is a technology, a communication system, as much and at times more than it is a system for organizing sexuality. It signals. Walk for a moment through a red-light district in your head and you won't see sex—just its red-hot flares.

Even the phrase "red-light district," as far as we know, comes from a communication practice, one said to originate with railroad men at the turn of the twentieth century. They would set their red signal lights down outside the doors of the women they'd hire between shifts in case their foremen needed to call them back to work.

Now when we hear tales about the red-light district, they most likely won't be coming from people who buy or sell sexual services. The red-light district you will hear about today is the province of the surveillance class—the police and the politicians, the researchers and the reporters. From their mouths, the online red-light district is rarely offered as a value-neutral term to describe a kind of commercial activity on the Internet: It's meant to convey what we're to understand as a troublesome growth and spread of commercial sex, though little evidence is offered for this alleged upsurge. It draws its evidence from a tautology that's appealing to those who can know only through surveillance: The Internet makes sex for sale easier to see, so the Internet must be increasing the number of people who buy and sell sex—because now we see more of them. The truth is we simply don't yet know how or even if the Internet has expanded markets for commercial sex. But it has certainly allowed many more outsiders to peep into them.

It's seductive to imagine that by being able to browse the

storefronts of sexually oriented businesses without leaving our homes and without being seen, we have access to some truth about commercial sex. Why flip through the ads in the back of the paper (and there aren't that many anymore, anyway) when you have the Web? You can click through LiveJasmin.com, where a mosaic of women's photos come to life as you mouse over them on the homepage, dozens of streaming video feeds of all the performers available wherever it is they are, and right here in the universal time zone of the live sex show.

Both the site design and the vicissitudes of the real live nude girl market mean that the mostly young women who've put out webcam shingles there seem to be always on and available. Some of the women look right at you (or at their webcams) but just as many look off to the side: They're not avoiding you, they're just absorbed in their computer screen, in something else to pass their unpaid time between the viewers buying private shows. (In the peep show, sex workers used the equivalent dead time to listen to the radio, and when customers made themselves known, they turned the boom box volume down with a toe while rearranging their bodies into an attentive pose.)

When the opportunity for voyeurism is your product, tolerating anyone's wandering eye without a dollar amount attached just feels like you're getting ripped off. There is a certain amount of show a performer must give for free, but there is a line, and each worker knows it, between the attentions of a prospective customer and the neediness of a time waster. To those interlocutors into sex businesses, those

would-be *flâneurs* with the mouse, particularly those who feel
that they should not or must not pay, will likely be treated as
the latter. Preserving one's propriety is no excuse. Having
something to offer—money—is what makes you a good citizen of the red-light district.

We could say that peep shows and porn theaters and street-
level sex work, particularly those conducted in mixed-use
neighborhoods, are being displaced by online ad directories
and live cam sites. But more to the point, the Web's sex
markets are flourishing in the vacant spaces left in the wake of
gentrification campaigns that imperiled the sex businesses
that also called those blocks home. These physical spaces are
gone, and may never be again: The anonymous sexual
encounter is now increasingly mediated by the digital.

That mediation only magnifies the power of myth making
about the online red-light district. It is no one fixed place but
a network of signs and solicitations. In the eighteenth century
we had the polite euphemism "public women" when it was
necessary to reference those who were presumed to be prostitutes. What public is left for the public women now? On the
flickering front page of LiveJasmin, the rest of the public can
imagine—as those equipped only with gaslight once imagined—the bodies upon which their illumination is cast were
just waiting for them to drop in a coin and bring them to life.

So it's all of this, not just the Internet, that drives the online
red-light district, to the extent that there even is one: the reliance on surveillance to know sex workers; the adoption of
online forms of solicitation; and the gentrification of concrete
red-light districts through policing and capital. This all means

that when we consider people who don't engage in commercial sex, who are most commonly known as the general public, they are far less likely to ever meet a sex worker in the physical world and are more likely than ever before to learn everything they know about sex work from marketing copy written for sex workers' customers.

In the age of the online red-light district, everyone's been made a john.

7
The Stigma

So why didn't I want to write this? Because there's so much written about the sex industry already. I know because before I started dancing, I read all that I could about it. Unfortunately, a lot of what's out there is misleading. Most of the literature either mystifies or demonizes sex work. There was nothing about what it was like or what it does to you . . . As much as I dislike identifying so strongly with anything I do for money, I have to write this. Maybe then I can write something else.

—Janet, *Rocket Queen* zine

It was whores who first theorized that all women live under the conditions of what they named "whore stigma." Proposed as a feminist intervention, whore stigma offers another reason why no universal female class exists. "The whore stigma," states Gail Pheterson in her 1996 essay of the same name in *The Prostitution Prism*, "attaches not to femaleness alone, but to illegitimate or illicit femaleness. In other words, being a woman is a pre-condition of the label 'whore' but never the sole justification."

Sex workers, along with many people who do not do sex work, are exposed to whore stigma for breaking with, or being perceived to have broken with, what Jill Nagle calls "compulsory virtue." It's a riff on Adrienne Rich's "compulsory heterosexuality," with which lesbians are made invisible. Whore stigma, Nagles writes, is "a mandate not only to *be* virtuous, but also to *appear* virtuous." As with compulsory heterosexuality, compulsory virtue isn't just about producing a set of behaviors (fucking men, being a good girl about it), but producing a system of social control (punishing queers, jailing whores). "One does not actually have to be a whore to suffer a whore's punishment or stigma," writes Nagle. Naming whore stigma offers us a way through it: to value difference, to develop solidarity between women in and out of the sex trade.

Along with the phrase sex work, whore stigma is situated in an explicit sex worker feminism, one that acknowledges that while only some women may be sex workers, all of us negotiate whore stigma. Whore solidarity actions predate that vocabulary, like the occupation of a London church in 1982 organized by the English Collective of Prostitutes (ECP). "We'd bought fifty black masks," writes Selma James, then the spokesperson for ECP. "In that way, prostitute and nonprostitute women would not be distinguishable from each other, and press photos of either would not be dangerous." Entering the church alongside them were identified members of the organizations Women Against Rape and Black Women for Wages for Housework. "We were uncertain of our safety," James writes, "and were glad to have two 'respectable' women's groups with us." Even those who are not whores can rise up with whores, can put their own respectability to work through their willingness to no longer be so closely identified with it.

This has been one of the foundational contributions of sex worker feminists to feminist discourse and activism: challenging whore stigma in the name of all those who live under it. There's an echo of this in the popularization of whore stigma in a milder form as outrage at "slut shaming." What is lost, however, in moving from whore stigma to slut shaming is the centrality of the people most harmed by this form of discrimination.

There is also an alarming air, in some feminists' responses to slut shaming, of assumed distance, that the fault in slut shaming is a sorting error: *No, she is certainly not a "slut"!* This preserves the slut as contemptible rather than focusing on those who attack women who violate compulsory virtue— for being too loud, too much, too opinionated, too black, too queer. *Slut* may seem to broaden the tent of those affected, but it makes the whore invisible. Whore stigma makes central the racial and class hierarchy reinforced in the dividing of women into the pure and the impure, the clean and the unclean, the white and virgin and all the others. If woman is other, whore is the other's other.

I'm thinking here of the first time I saw a SlutWalk protest, in Las Vegas in the summer of 2006, during the century's first national gathering of sex workers activists. SlutWalk hadn't been invented yet. It would be another four years before Toronto police officer Michael Sanguinetti explained to a group of university women, with the kind of contempt not unfamiliar to sex workers, that "women should avoid dressing like sluts in order not to be victimized." SlutWalk, in its way, was also a reaction to police harassment, though one raised by women who presumed, unlike the prostitutes of San Francisco and London, that the police would listen to them in the first place.

It should not be surprising that the first vocal critics of SlutWalk were women of color and women in the sex trade. Reading the SlutWalk rallying cry, writes Brittney Cooper of *Crunk Feminist Collective*:

> I was struck by the righteous indignation these women had over being called slut. Although plenty of Black women have been called "slut," I believe Black women's histories are different, in that Black female sexuality has always been understood from without to be deviant, hyper, and excessive.

For some white women, slut transgresses a boundary they've never imagined crossing. Women of color, working-class women, queer women: They were never presumed to have that boundary to begin with.

In Vegas, on the sex workers' own walk, protesters dressed in the kinds of costumes we now associate with SlutWalk— fishnets, leather and PVC corset tops, shiny hot pants, tall boots, and platform heels—with wild hair and hand-painted signs and slogans on their chests and stomachs (another homage to an older feminist practice: to riot grrrl, or at least to the photographs that had circulated of riot grrrl, few of the protesters having been around to be riot grrrls themselves). Marching from casino to casino, sex workers took over the carefully sculpted Vegas sidewalks, passing out fliers to tourists and to the few sex workers who were also out that night although, since they were working, attired far more conservatively. Dressed and brazenly conducting themselves as they never could if they were actually working the tables and lounges for clients, the protesters were more shocking to the men employed by the casinos and hotels to surveil, who came and went, and at Caesars, despite the intervention of a lawyer from the ACLU who had tagged along with the march, were hustled out. It's not that they were whores, as clearly whores are permitted in Vegas casinos. It's how the space they took up put whoring in the public's face; that's why they were removed.

At the Wynn, on my way up to a party following the sex work conference a few nights before, with activist and artist Sadie Lune and an outreach worker from St. James Infirmary, a sex worker health clinic, an elevator attendant stopped us, asking if we were there for "a party." "We are," we said, "but . . ." and he began to explain, kindly, that if we had called ahead he could have made arrangements for us to be taken up in the VIP elevator. "No, no, we're not here for," one of us started to explain, "that kind of party . . ." which then would have to be followed up with, ". . . not that there's anything wrong with that"—and not that he was wrong about us—"but . . ." so instead we just left it there, and went up the elevator meant for everyone but the whores.

"What it was like and what it does to you."

When the public is groomed to expect a poor, suffering whore, it's appreciable why some sex workers who do come out take pains to provide a counternarrative: to never look like a prostitute. They are asked only to talk about how empowering it all was or about how much of a survivor they are. They have to convince their audiences how much they always had their shit together, how they do now—how they are not like those *other girls*, whoever they are.

Sometimes, like when calling out "slut shaming" only to then shame sluts, this undermines solidarity. This is just rearranging the pecking order of sex and gender outcasts rather than refusing to order ourselves in the first place. There's a risk of reinventing the virgin/whore hierarchy within sex work, even when—to everyone else—all of us could still be whores.

Telling the truth can exact collective costs. When each sex worker's story carries with it the demands of correcting this whole historic record, each comes preopposed. "It's not just *Pretty Woman!*" someone will complain, as if anyone but a few movie PR people ever claimed that. "Well," they go on, "they're not all *Happy Hookers!*" but neither was the real-life happy hooker. Read Xaviera Hollander's 1972 bestseller, and you won't set foot in her brothel without first being led through shabby and unsatisfying apartments and relationships and nasty men posing as nasty cops conspiring to stalk and extort the author. The people most responsible for keeping the myth of the happy hooker alive are in fact those who are so convinced of their misery.

Remember also the teacher who appeared on the cover of the *New York Post* in late 2010, who was photographed without her knowledge on her way to work. Along with the pictures the *Post* dubbed her "the hooker teacher," shaming her for publishing an essay criticizing the campaign to shutdown Craigslist's sex work ads and making reference to her previous work as an escort. She hadn't always enjoyed her job, she wrote, but it had been her job, and Craigslist had been her way to have that job on more of her own terms. The teacher, Melissa Petro, had never told her students she was a sex worker, or discussed sex work in her classroom. There had never been complaints about her performance. It was the *Post* photos and the headlines that got her "reassigned to administrative duties" and ultimately dismissed from her job.

You would think that the kinds of women's groups who lobby for the abolition of sex work would have risen to Melissa Petro's defense. She had talked openly and honestly about her past, including the times it felt as if escorting damaged her sense of self. She had left sex work for a low-paying job as a teacher, moving on with her life. But she had also written about why shutting down Craigslist's Erotic Services section could be harmful for sex workers. Those same anti–sex work women's groups that normally might defend a woman wrongly fired from her job were spearheading the campaign to close Erotic Services, so they were silent.

As a whore regarded by the public, there is no right way to be a victim.

A few months after the *Post* had moved on from Melissa Petro's story, and while she was still fighting to find another job in the wake of the coverage, I was standing on the edge of a parking lot on Gilgo Beach on Long Island, NY. The family members of women whose bodies had been found there had organized a press conference marking the discovery of another body: the remains of Shannan Gilbert. Ten bodies had been found by now, five of them women who had once used Craigslist or Backpage and had gone missing in the course of

seeing customers. The families of the other missing women—
Megan Waterman, Melissa Barthelemy, Maureen Brainard-
Barnes, and Amber Lynn Costello—had met one another as
their missing daughters' and sisters' stories hit the press. They
shared tips and information with each other. They started a
Facebook page to draw out more leads, to keep the story alive.

Maybe there were two dozen people there that day, counting the families, a lawyer, supporters, and the news crews.
There was no way of knowing from watching the video
report later how many of us were actually there. The Gilbert
family clustered together in front of the microphones. The
cameras were a good distance away. The family spoke more
to the people who weren't there than to those of us who were,
shivering in the winter wind lashing at the shoreline. They
wept and vowed to find out the truth, begged people with
information to come forward, offered a reward, speculated
about when the FBI might get involved—which they didn't,
and as far as anyone knows, they still haven't.

"I can't imagine doing this over and over," I told Audacia Ray,
who runs a media advocacy organization for and by sex workers
called the Red Umbrella Project, who had driven a group of us
out there. We met in 2004, after exchanging comments on each
other's blogs. Now we were living in the same city and were both
retired from sex work, and I was reporting and Dacia was there to
help the families, if they wanted it, through talking to the press.
Doing this each time they find a body, crying for all these cameras.
It was like their currency. It's what they've got left.

Dacia told me that, in a way, it was worse than that. There
weren't as many cameras today as there were the last time.

8

The Other Women

When the sex war is won prostitutes should be shot as collaborators for their terrible betrayal of all women.
— Julie Burchill, *Damaged Goods* (1989)

For the study, they recruited young women to wear bikinis. To document the effects of what they call "self-objectification," first, they asked the women to complete a set of math problems. Another group of women wearing sweaters were given the same problem set. Observing that some of the young women had a harder time with the math while wearing less clothing (and perhaps anticipating a researcher would soon return with yet more questions) researchers concluded that self-objectification was harmful to women. The American Psychological Association offered these results as part of a larger 2007 report, presented as evidence that "thinking about the body and comparing it to sexualized cultural ideals disrupted mental capacity." The APA's interpretation was greeted by some women's groups as welcome proof—but of what? That math is real work, whereas trying on bikinis is stressful? Of no scientific interest, when evaluating nudity's impact on self-esteem are all the actual women who perform essential feats of accounting while wearing G-strings, nightly. (Not—please—to incite a rush on strip clubs for such research.)

It's not an accident that even the arithmetic of sex workers is suspect. They are at once blamed for contributing to the objectification of women through being objectified themselves and, through their occupation, for sexualizing all women, and for profit. Writer Pamela Paul deemed this phenomenon "pornification," one in which the conventions of commercial sex are polluting all sexual relations. This is how women are transformed into "female chauvinist pigs," according to journalist Ariel Levy. If women participate in any form of sexual exhibitionism, they aren't pursuing their own fantasies but just playing into men's hands, stoking demand for this kind of "faking it," stimulating demand for whores while at the same time rendering them redundant by driving all women to whorishness. One woman's ruin is made all women's ruin.

For opponents of sexualization, the danger is not only that a woman will be reduced to a sexual being for the enjoyment of others, but that if a woman is sexualized, it obliterates her as *a real woman*—that is, it is a violence that renders her a lesser woman, a whore. At the root of the opposition to sexualization is the essential belief that for a woman to be thought of as a whore is so profoundly damaging that it constitutes a challenge to one's real womanhood.

This is where concerns about the sexualization of women

become inseparable from those conventional ideas about their sexual value, even though sexualization's critics claim to stand against the latter. "Thinking about the body" in a way the APA described as "sexual" in its report is what they claim "disrupted mental capacity." Rather than discourage young women from "thinking about the body" sexually, perhaps we should ask why how one feels about one's body in a bikini is an acceptable measure for evaluating any young woman's thoughts about her body and her sexuality, or why—again— the body is coded as the source of our self-worth. Developing women's sense of self-worth and sexuality isn't really the point of disrupting sexualization. "Perhaps the most insidious consequence of self-objectification," the researchers caution, "is that it fragments consciousness." Forget embracing your desires, girls; just swap the bikini for a sweater and the psychic wounds of patriarchy will be healed.

Confusing a representation of sex with sex itself is what sexualization's critics are supposed to stand against. These concerns about sexualization, focused as they are on image and fantasy, ignore the labor involved in performing sexual fantasy, the skills that enable sex workers to perform a fantasy without living it. Their worries begin to sound like a panic, a fear that the wrong kinds of sexual looks and wants must be confined or else all women may be at risk.

This isn't to deny that objectification and sexualization exist; this is to protest the narrowness of this focus, its potential to recast women as pure and blank slates who risk contamination from the wrong fantasies, the wrong desires. Resisting sexualization doesn't necessarily translate into greater sexual agency for women, and without a complementary demand for women's freedom, sexual and otherwise, this resistance can become a platform to defend women's absence from sexuality. In insisting that some representations of sexuality are less real (or more harmful, since these are used interchangeably) than others, boundaries between women, between desires, between classes of women and our labor are reinforced.

Porn and stripping get the rap for driving sexualization, though critiques of them only go as far as representations of our labor—the pole, the thong, the waxed pussy—and not to our labor itself, not to our lives. Critics get close to the truth: Acting as if we share our customers' desires is the work of sex work. But that's not the same as allowing our customers to define our sexuality. When critics do venture outside the representational, it's to insist that sex workers are victims of sexualization, that they are responsible for the sexualization of all women. This is a return to older claims that sex workers suffer from "false consciousness," only now with a dash of social science and perhaps in tinier underwear than was available to the second wave.

To see off-the-clock sex workers as whole, as people who aren't just here to fuck, would defy sexualization. But that's not the role they're permitted, especially by the women who seek to save them.

Pornographic Feeling

Fears of sexualization and pornification are nothing new, and as in earlier waves of contempt for porn's gaze, the fears quickly becomes contempt for people in the sex trade. The late seventies and early eighties were the heyday of Women Against Pornography (WAP)—a backlash, in many ways, to the increased visibility of sex workers in the women's movement. Just a few years after the National Organization for Women invited her to present a slide show on women and masturbation in 1973, artist and sex educator Betty Dodson participated in one of WAP's group meetings in New York; she later wrote that it was impossible to imagine the NOW slide show happening in the climate produced by WAP. At the WAP event, woman after woman went to the podium and recounted stories of how porn had injured her. "Each speaker's words and tears were firing up the room into a unified rage," Dodson writes in her essay "Porn Wars" in *The Feminist Porn Book*.

Rather than egalitarian consciousness-raising, the sharing of stories took on an air of sentimental performance. "An attractive blonde in her midthirties stood at the mic," writes Dodson. "With her rage barely controlled, she described her childhood sexual abuse," which involved her father using what the woman called "disgusting, filthy pictures" and her being made to perform an "unnatural act." Dodson remembers, "The whole room was emotionally whipped up into a rage with their own private images of child rape, while at the same time, reveling in the awfulness of it." If this is how porn's relationship to women is understood, how is any woman who dissents—let alone one who has modeled for pictures—supposed to speak for herself without speaking against the violation of this child? How are you to say that the description of the child's violation by a woman on a stage itself mimes a pornographic revelation? How is this group of women's consumption of the evil of pornography in a group exhibition all that different from the men seated in a Times Square theater having their own communal experience of porn?

There is a sameness here to the communal release of feeling, the shaking of the body whether consumed by sobs or ejaculations: This is what film theorist Linda Williams saw in her analysis of porn films and "weepies"—chick flicks. To be in these rooms of women raging against pornography is to give in to the hawker's sidewalk promise of "hardcore" relief. The women whose relationship to pornography has never included participating in it are only incidentally concerned with the actual women in it. Though they claim some relationship to the women in pornography, it's one only to pictures of their bodies, to these bodies as they are made occupants of the viewers' own imagination. The passionate antiporn campaigner has this much in common with the avid porn consumer.

This sexualized portrayal we're supposed to be outraged about is not limited to pornography; it's also in the iconography of the contemporary antiprostitution movement. In images on billboards and posters in social service agencies, and traded on Facebook and Pinterest to demonstrate membership in this movement, women are shown in shadow, bent over, in heels, in short skirts, wide-eyed, bruised, and chained, their open mouths covered by the hands of men— often those of faceless men of color. For a group so focused on finding evidence of the violence done to women in media imagery, they produce their own fair share, playing to the same tropes. Perhaps it's intentional, to garner attention—a pseudosubversive gimmick. Still, it takes on a perverse air, when, for example, a campaign called Fresh Meat from Reden International in Denmark that decries sex slavery brands itself with an image of a half-dozen nude women folded at the waist with their knees drawn up to their chests, all arranged in a styrofoam tray and sheathed in plastic wrap. I'm loathe to use a word they've thoroughly demeaned, but to see women this way is dehumanizing.

Against Real Women

But what if being sexualized is neither dehumanizing nor empowering, and is simply value neutral? That the harms here reside not in the looking or feeling but in what actually impacts the body? Should women be more concerned that men want to fuck us or to fuck us and fuck us up? These (sex workers still find themselves insisting) are not the same.

This is why the concerns of the real women in the sex industry do not fully register with opponents, if they do at all. If, as Burchill writes, the prostitute stands in opposition to "all women," that's a neat way of explaining why she can be ignored, as she must no longer be a woman herself. This boundary is drawn each time sex workers are told that by virtue of their labor they have been "reduced" to objects. They're told they're blameless, as the opponents don't actually value this labor, and instead they put the blame on customers, on men's eyes and desires.

The goal, these antiprostitute advocates say, of eradicating men's desire for paid sex isn't "antisex" but to restore the personhood of prostitutes, that is, of people who are already people except to those who claim to want to fix them. Prostitutes, in their imagination, have actually become the mute objects men have reduced them to. They are apparently unlike all other women, who face objectification but can retain the ability to speak and move in the world independently.

Sex workers know they are objectified; they move in the world as women too, and through their work they have to become fluent in the narrow and kaleidoscopic visions through which men would like to relate to them as sexual fantasies embodied. They know they also serve as objects of fantasy for women: as the bad girls to fear and keep far from and, on occasion, to furtively imagine themselves as.

It's objectification, too, when these "supporters" represent sex workers as degraded, as victims, and as titillating object lessons, and render sex workers' whole selves invisible. Their capacity for social relations is dismissed, their lives under-stood to be organized almost entirely around what others call their sexual availability and what sex workers call their labor.

Witholding Consent

Sex work is not simply sex; it is a performance, it is playing a role, demonstrating a skill, developing empathy within a set of professional boundaries. All this could be more easily recognized and respected as labor were it the labor of a nurse, a therapist, or a nanny. To insist that sex work is work is also to affirm there is a difference between a sexualized form of labor and sexuality itself.

Opponents attack sex workers who view their work in this way. "The only analogy I can think of concerning prostitution is that it is more like gang rape than it is like anything else," antiporn feminist Andrea Dworkin offered in a lecture at the University of Michigan Law School in 1992. "The gang rape is punctuated by a money exchange. That's all. That's the only difference." Taking it a bit further, antiprostitution activist Evelina Giobbe refers to prostitution, in a publication of the same name, as "buying the right to rape." If this is a right, why must men purchase it?

When anti–sex work activists claim that all sex work is rape, they don't just ignore the labor; they excuse the actual rape of sex workers. If men can do whatever they want when they buy sex, the rape of sex workers, of those who are thought to have no consent to give anyway, isn't understood by opponents as an aberration but as somehow intrinsic and inevitable.

Consent in sex work, as in noncommercial sex, is more complex than a simple binary yes/no contract. Sex workers negotiate based not only on a willingness to perform a sex act but on the conditions under which their labor is performed:

Yes, I will give you a lap dance for $20. If you want me to stay for another song after the first one has ended, it will be another $20. If you want your dance in the private room, that will be $150.

Or:

> I'll come to your motel room for a half an hour, and that
> will cost $150. If you want me to strip, you need to tip me,
> and tips start at $50. If you want me to give you a massage,
> that's $100 tip.

Or maybe:

> I'll give you a blow job in your car for $40, but you need to
> drive over to this spot (where I know my friends can write
> down your license plate, and they know that I will be leav-
> ing your car as soon as you come, and if you drive away
> before I get out they will know something is wrong and
> come after me).

The presence of money does not remove one's ability to consent. Consent, in and out of sex work, is not just given but constructed, and from multiple factors: setting, time, emotional state, trust, *and* desire. Desire is contingent on all of these. Consent and desire aren't states frozen in our bodies, tapped into and felt or offered. They are formed.

Money, rather than serving as a tangible symbol of consent, clarifies that consent to any sexual interaction isn't a token given from one person to another like a few bills changing hands. Money is just one factor, even if it is in many cases the most important one, in constructing consent.

It would be a mistake, then, to confuse desire with consent. There is much that sex workers do in their work that they will not enjoy doing, and yet they do consent and have legitimate reasons for doing so. Writer and prostitute Charlotte Shane terms this "unenthusiastic consent," a flip of the recent feminist call to demand "enthusiastic consent," a "yes means yes" to fight for alongside "no means no." Shane isn't saying yes means no, but rather, as she writes at the blog *Tits and Sass*, "There is a stark difference between the times I've agreed to (undesired) sex with clients, and the times I haven't agreed to certain types of sex with clients. Labeling all of those experiences 'rape' erases the truth, my reality, and my agency." We have an understanding now, through the advocacy of feminist antirape activists, that even when our consent is violated, we can feel (despite ourselves?) pleasure. The corollary, then, is that pleasure isn't necessary for one to have offered consent, and the absence of pleasure should not be construed as a withdrawal of consent.

If rape isn't just bad sex, just bad sex—even at work—isn't rape.

But maybe it's a distraction to talk about something like consent to sex at all when we talk about sexual labor. There is a whole matrix of consent to consider: Will the sexual labor performed put one at risk of law enforcement? At a health risk? At risk for being outed? It's those conditions that deserve as much if not more of our concern when considering consent, not just consent to a sex act. Focusing on consent to sex may do more to perpetuate confusion and marginalization than clarifying sex workers' power and control at work.

Isolating sex workers' consent to only sexual consent is used to diminish their choices, not enhance them. Sex workers, more than any other, are expected to justify their labor as a choice, as if the choice to engage in a form of labor is what makes that labor legitimate. An even more insidious double standard is that sex workers must prove they have made an *empowered* choice, as if empowerment is some intangible state attained through self-perfection and not through a continuous and collective negotiation of power. These demands to demonstrate one's empowerment only reproduces a victim class among sex workers, all of whom are already perceived to be disempowered. It's as true of sex workers as it is for nurses or teachers (or journalists or academics): Dwelling on the individual capacity for empowerment does little to help uncover the systemic forces constraining workers' power, on the job and off.

> I've "sold my body" to countless men yet I still have it right here on the couch with me. Odd that.
>
> —@AnarchaSxworker

Following from these myths—that to be objectified is to reduce the self, and that sex for pay is indistinguishable from rape—are the two common and contradictory views of what a sex worker sells: either her body or herself, which is most commonly applied to sex workers who offer a physical service, traditional straight sex in particular; or a shoddy approximation of real sex, making her a fake.

Drawing from over a decade of ethnographic study, sociologist Elizabeth Bernstein identifies what sex workers offer as bounded intimacy, a service that can contain a range of labor, from the physical to the emotional. Some sex workers, particularly those whose service allows for extended conversation with customers (whether over an hour-long hotel encounter, a webcam chat, or in VIP rooms), may negotiate their work quite differently than those who prefer to focus on the physical labor of sex, which can be a more straightforward service. Sex workers don't all find the same physical sex acts equally intimate: a blow job, a massage, a strap-on ass fuck, a kiss.

That sex workers are continually negotiating varying levels of intimacy should be proof enough that this is labor rather than selling one's body. But that the intimacy itself can be constructed might seem like evidence that what's on offer can't be real. Still, we judge sex workers' authenticity by much higher standards than we might, for example, judge the connection we have with a favorite bartender, a hair stylist, or even a therapist—when, actually, we might prefer a bit of distance, and understand that that is part of the point.

Negotiating authenticity isn't just the domain of sex work. Bernstein relates the emergence of bounded intimacy to the broader transition to the service economy from industrial labor. In an economy in which workers of all kinds are called on to produce an experience—not just a coffee, but a smile and a personal greeting; not just a vacation, but a spiritual retreat—sex work fits quite comfortably.

Brents, Jackson, and Hausbeck, in their study of Nevada's brothels, for example, describe how some of these workplaces are defined not just as sexual escapes but as escapes from the workaday world into a conventionally feminine environment. It's not only the sexual performance that will attract a customer but the performance of leisure and comfort—not unlike the luxury vacation resort, where customers are offered a comprehensive experience of escape.

After Sexualization

Critics miss the ways in which the sex economy is working to mainstream itself in their shallow focus on sexualization: not to sexualize the mainstream, but the other way around. As the researchers observed, raunch isn't used to appeal to the mainstream in the Nevada brothels, but they instead market themselves as classy and upscale, as the kind of places anyone might want to experience. It's the mainstream leisure industry in Las Vegas—where brothels are not permitted—that plays up the sinfulness of sex appeal. This interplay is what they describe not as a sexualization of culture but as a convergence.

When opponents of sexualization and sex work do take aim at those who profit from women's images, their attack can be narrow and reactionary. Critics misread the interconnections between the mainstream and sex economies and media as one of contamination rather than coexistence, and so they lack the ability or will to situate sexual images in the market or the wider social sphere. Simply removing the visible top layer of our sexually converged economy will not go far at all to changing what sexualization is said to reinforce: the fundamental inequities of the rest of the economy. These campaigns start and end with erasing women's bodies.

If we take the naked girl out of the picture in *Playboy* or on

Page 3, it does nothing to free any of us from the constraints on women's actual sexual lives, on our power. To remove so-called sexy images from view in the supermarket, the Internet, wherever they are said to do the most damage becomes a quick, soundbite-y substitute for the kinds of demands we might make if we shifted our attention off the exposed skin and onto the lives of those women off the screen, off the clock.

The incoherence of these arguments is most evident in complaints that women in sex work are somehow responsible for the desire of women outside the industry to act like them, and for free. No other generation of young women, Levy claims in *Female Chauvinist Pigs*, have grown up "when porn stars weren't topping the bestseller charts, when strippers weren't mainstream"—as if making icons of sex workers were confined to the twenty-first century (ask the courtesans of Venice, the burlesque queens of old), or the public's embrace of pop representations of sex work is the same as embracing sex workers. "The thong," she warns, "is the literal by-product of the sex industry," as if this is reason enough to cast them out, as if this is what holds us back. The thong and the women who first wore them are interchangeable for Levy, and interchangeable, too, with actual male dominance. They mistake the sex workers' whole selves, as they accuse men of doing, with their uniform for the day.

Objects in the Rear View May Appear

Sex workers are only a symbol for Levy and other "raunch culture" opponents, a symptom of some more important

disease who matter only insofar as they impact the behavior
of other women, the women who matter. I could say that
their analysis is flawed, that it confines our understanding of
sex to the representational and how it makes women feel
(often, about other women) rather than to the material and
how it constrains and shapes our lives, but that is precisely
the point: Sex work informs their analysis of sexualization
not because sex workers' lives are important but because sex
work makes women who don't do it feel things they prefer
not to feel. It is the whore stigma exercised and upheld by
other women.

How different might our analysis of the relationship
between sex, value, and womanhood be if we could see
through the panic of sexualization to the tectonic social and
economic shifts that have pushed commercial sex and its
representations to the surface? If we let go of the desire to
diagnose and pathologize what's been called sexualization,
we could observe and describe women's lives more fully and
describe more precisely how power and sex shape us.

The convergence of commercial sex with service economies gives a way to understand what looks like the main-
streaming of commercial sex; it also provides an alternative
framework to sexualization for understanding this transformation. This frees us from having to position commercial or
noncommercial sex as the "right" choice, since it locates
commercial sex on a continuum of other commercial services—travel, beauty, dining, entertainment—that we don't
feel we have to judge as better or worse than their noncommercial counterparts before coming to an analysis of their

value. It doesn't regard sex work as service work in order to imagine what it could be: It acknowledges that sex work and service work already overlap, share workforces, and are interdependent.

By extension, valuing the ability of sex workers to negotiate intimacy can shift the focus of those who seek to end sex workers' exploitation: from representations of sexualization to the ways sex workers' labor is organized. When massive chains like Pret A Manger or Starbucks require their workers to serve up coffee with a smile or else, we don't believe we can remedy this demand for forced niceties by telling attention-desperate customers to get their emotional needs met elsewhere. The demand lies not with the customers' whims, but with the management. This is why sex workers gain no greater control over their work by locating their exploitation only or even primarily in the hands of their customers. It's understandable why that might be appealing, in an age where consumer choice is seen as the salve on so many labor abuses. Buying "the right things" might matter, but not enough, and not much at all at the bargaining table.

It's doubly appealing to blame commercial sex consumers when your concerns about commercial sex have less to do with the health and wellbeing of sex workers than with, as Burchill and Dworkin and their supporters have demanded, the wholesale eradication of their livelihood. Sex workers' own needs, in contrast, should be quite a bit more familiar to all women: to be legally recognized; to end discrimination in housing, health care, education, and work; to move freely in the world. Even for those who wish to leave the sex trade, their demands to seek an alternative income would hardly be met by the elimination of their current one.

As controlled by customer demand as sex workers are supposed to be, anti–sex work reformers carry on far more about customers than sex workers do, insisting that they and their sexual demands are all-powerful. Sex workers are made helpless before them, their consent and critical thinking apparently eroded by their attire. The advocates won't say we were asking for it, but they still claim to know better than we do. Is it out of fear that they might someday have to do the same, to cross the hard line they imagine divides them from the "other" women?

9
The Saviors

As far as Western media is concerned, the foremost expert on sex work in Cambodia is Nicholas Kristof. It doesn't hurt that he works for the *New York Times* and that his position on sex work aligns with that of the American and Cambodian governments, who would like it "eradicated." This is also what permitted him to "purchase" two women who worked in brothels in Poipet. If he had been operating as a private citizen, he could have been charged as a trafficker or a sex tourist. A press badge, along with his proper readership, protected him.

Kristof has gone to Cambodia bearing and promising both police and rescue, as nongovernmental organizations (NGO) sometimes do: While riding shotgun along with international antiprostitution NGO the Somaly Mam Foundation on a brothel raid in northern Cambodia, he broadcast what he saw for his audience on Twitter, a breathless stream detailing people he described as scared, underage rape victims. It goes without saying that he published all of this without obtaining their consent.

Police burst in, disarmed brothel owners, took their
phones so they can't call for help . . . Girls are rescued, but
still very scared. Youngest looks about 13, trafficked from
Vietnam . . . Social workers comforting the girls, telling
them they are free, won't be punished, rapes are over.

—@NickKristof

Kristof is not alone in this peculiar participatory literary
tradition of exposing this heart of darkness that is prostitution: At the turn of the last century, William T. Stead used his
column inches in London's *Pall Mall Gazette* to drum up
concern over a burgeoning "white slave trade" that never
quite turned up to be documented. Not that this stopped him:
Stead did time as a result of the story for which he had bought
a thirteen-year-old, the sacrificial heroine of his exposé enti-
tled "The Maiden Tribute of Modern Babylon." He only
went to jail because he bought the girl from her mother rather
than her father, who was understood to have had a legal right
to her.

The panic Stead helped stir up got a new antiprostitution
law passed in the United Kingdom, and would soon drift
across the Atlantic; states from Iowa to California drew up
"red-light abatement acts," the beginning of the end of toler-
ated prostitution in the United States. All of them were prem-
ised on fears that our nation's (white) daughters were doomed
to a life of waste, to be held captive in the "modern Babylon"
of industrial capital.

We might say that people like Kristof have erred in mythol-
ogizing sex work using only its worst cases, but we aren't in a

position to know what the concept of worst cases even means to those who adhere to this tradition, which casts all sex work as a worst case merely for existing. This allegedly honest storytelling cannot accommodate the range of experiences sex workers have, report on, and are adamant about having understood.

Such a vision of sex work is easily communicable. The December 2012 newsletter of the Kolkata-based, US-registered antiprostitution group Apne Aap published an account from a new volunteer, what she had deduced only from the few minutes of her first guided tour through Sonagachi, Kolkata's red-light district:

> There are more than just brothels here; facing the streets are stores, homes, businesses and shops. People live, work, and carry out ordinary lives in Sonagachi, too. Some of the girls we saw were dressed in average clothing, weren't wearing any make-up, and may have been out living everyday lives. But it wasn't long before I saw what we had come to witness, a group of prostituted girls that couldn't have been older than fifteen or sixteen. They were standing outside a doorway, waiting. Waiting for purchase. They were dressed up, wearing their colorful saris, had make-up on their faces, and their skin was fair, as that is a highly demanded quality. All these efforts are an attempt to make the girls look healthy and happy to be there, however, the girls were not well. You could easily tell by their faces and from their sunken eyes that they were tired, ill and sick with disease and trauma . . . It was

impossible not to look at the girls, just standing there waiting. Waiting for the next person to dehumanize her, to
rape her, to take away more of her childhood. That's all
she is, a teenage girl disguised as an adult to fulfill the
desire of someone who's buying the domination of another
human being. The fear and terror of living in this hell is
immeasurable.

The experience of sex work is more than just the experience of
violence; to reduce all sex work to such an experience is to
deny that anything but violence is even possible. By doing so,
there is no need to listen to sex workers; if we already know
their fate, their usefulness lies solely in providing more
evidence for the readers' preconceptions. For those working
in the antiprostitution rescue industry, sex workers are limited
to performing as stock characters in a story they are not otherwise a part of, in the pity porn which the "expert" journalists,
filmmakers, and NGO staff will produce, profit from, and
build their power on. Meanwhile, when sex workers do face
discrimination, harassment, or violence, these can be explained
away as experiences intrinsic to sex work—and therefore,
however horrifically, to be expected. Though this antiprostitution perspective claims to be more sympathetic to sex workers, it produces the same ideology as the usual distrust and
discarding of them: Both claim that abuse comes with the
territory in sex work. If a sex worker reports a rape, well, what
did she expect?

I have not worked as a sex worker in Cambodia, so my
knowledge is limited to what I've observed firsthand, what

others have told me, and what I have found comparing the various official publications of governments with the NGOs who attempt to uncover abuses. But what I have that Nicholas Kristof does not is trust. Through my relationships with sex workers and sex worker activists in the United States, I met several from Cambodia. When I visited a brothel outside Phnom Penh, it was at their invitation, with no grand welcome or melodramatic conclusion.

Arriving with activists and outreach workers, we were greeted by sex workers who weren't otherwise occupied, dropped off some boxes of condoms, and then gathered in an open courtyard. They brought us cold scented cloths with which to dab our faces and pitchers of water. I didn't bring a camera crew, unlike NBC's *Dateline,* or countless well-meaning documentary filmmakers. Nor did we bring the police and the promise of rescue. Instead, we sat together on plastic patio chairs under the stars and talked there, openly.

Back in my hotel room in Phnom Penh there was a sign in English on the door, posted where I could read it in bed: SEX WORKERS ARE STRICTLY FORBIDDEN IN THE HOTEL. I could look out across the road from my window, swollen with motorbikes and *tuk-tuk* traffic at sunset, passing by the river where the Women's Network for Unity (WNU) office's boat was docked. Earlier I had sat on its wooden floor with a few of their members, circled around a MacBook, watching videos they'd made themselves and were posting on YouTube.

As we watched videos—stop-motion animations that used Barbie dolls in the roles of sex workers who wanted to remain anonymous but still speak out, and another, a work-in-progress about the abuse of mandatory health-check programs to extort bribes from workers—banners hung overhead moved gently in the breeze coming in off the water: DON'T TALK TO ME ABOUT SEWING MACHINES. TALK TO ME ABOUT WORKERS' RIGHTS.

The hit was a karaoke video, a slide show of images casting then US secretary of state Condoleezza Rice as Mary Magdalene in *Jesus Christ Superstar*, singing "I Don't Know How to Love Him" as a troubled ballad directed to President George W. Bush. At the time the State Department was pressuring the Cambodian government to take a stand against sex work or else lose aid from the United States Agency for International Development (USAID). Cambodian police, who had long been cracking down on sex workers, were now working in concert with the Ministry of Social Affairs, Veterans, and Youth Rehabilitation; they were hauling sex workers out of brothels, loading them onto the backs of trucks en route to "rehabilitation" centers. They didn't anticipate that sex workers would snap photos of these raids on their cell phones. One of these pictures showed up on placards and on buttons made by the Asia Pacific Network of Sex Workers (APNSW), with USAID renamed "USRAID."

What happened once the sex workers rounded up in brothel raids were unloaded from the trucks and moved to the so-called rehabilitation centers? They were illegally detained for months at a time without charges, as were others who worked in public parks and had been chased, beaten, and dragged into vans by police. The Cambodian human rights organization LICADHO captured chilling photographs of sex workers caught in sweeps locked together in a cage—thirty or forty people in one cell. Sex workers who had been detained reported being beaten and sexually assaulted by guards in interviews with LICADHO, Women's Network for Unity, and Human Rights Watch. Some living with HIV, who had been illegally held in facilities described by the local NGOs that ran them as "shelters," were denied access to antiretroviral medication. In one facility sex workers were "only able to leave their rooms to bathe twice a day in dirty pond water," Human Rights Watch reported, "or, accompanied by a guard, to go to the toilet."

The Asia Pacific Network of Sex Workers reported that a common theme in interviews with detainees was the appalling food delivered in plastic bags which they then retained to use as toilets, disposing of them by hurling them from windows. Through eyewitness accounts, human rights observers established that at least three detainees were beaten to death by guards. Observers from LICADHO witnessed the body of one woman, left to die after advocates found her just the day before comatose on the floor of a detention room where she had been locked in with twenty other people. This occured at a facility on Koh Kor, an island that had once served as a prison under the Khmer Rouge. "The government needs to find real solutions to the economic and social problems which cause people to live and work on the streets," LICADHO stated in their 2008 report on conditions at Koh Kor and a second facility at Prey Speu. "It cannot simply round these people up and throw them into detention camps."

If the sex workers standing in the doorways in Phnom Penh's red-light district looked out on the street with fear, it could be just as likely from the prospect of rescue as due to any customer.

As is the case for much of industry, accurate data on how many sex workers are in Cambodia are hard to come by and difficult to trust. One study USAID funded themselves found that of a sample of roughly 20,000, 88 percent were not forced into sex work, whether through physical force or debt contracts. It's especially tough to know how accurate figures on coercion are. But these are the figures found in the USAID-commissioned study and were presumably available to all those in the State Department who were agitating for crackdowns on all Cambodian sex work as a means to end trafficking.

These crackdowns are no corrective to abusive conditions in sex work, and can expose sex workers to yet more abuse, including those who want out. But this is of no concern to the American government, which not only wishes to "eradicate prostitution" (as a US attorney testified on USAID's behalf before the US Supreme Court in 2013), but requires those receiving foreign aid to agree with them. When the Cambodian government sought to demonstrate their commitment to these American values, they had in no way "eradicated prostitution"—they had simply taken action, through detention and violence, to eradicate sex workers themselves. The State Department, in turn, upgraded Cambodia's compliance ranking, and in its 2010 *Trafficking in Persons Report*, offered only a weak admonishment that "raids against 'immoral' activities were not conducted in a manner sensitive to trafficking victims," and recommend further "training," not investigations or sanctions. The US has spoken: They see no meaningful difference between the elimination of sex work and the elimination of sex workers themselves.

"The twin assumptions that no woman would willingly sell sex and that sex workers lack education and skills for 'decent' work are central to the issues playing out in Cambodia," writes Cheryl Overs, author of the 2009 APNSW report *Caught Between the Tiger and the Crocodile: The Campaign to Suppress Human Trafficking and Sexual Exploitation in Cambodia*. In truth, many have also worked in garment factories, and left the factories due to low wages to move into sex work. The APNSW logo, a sewing machine with a red circle and slash through it, is a nod to all of this. Although antiprostitution NGOs such as International Justice Mission and AFESIP (the Somaly Mam Foundation) claim to teach women they have "rescued" and "recovered" from brothels to operate sewing machines at their Cambodian shelters, sex and garment workers together call attention to the poor conditions in the factories that make sex work a higher-paying, more attractive alternative.

It was these workers, under the umbrella of WNU and APNSW, who came out strongly protesting against the crackdowns and illegal detentions in the summer of 2008. Sex workers told their stories of detention and abuse at the hands of police and guards at a rally in Phnom Penh of 500 of their colleagues and hundreds of allies. They screened video testimony from others who had been denied medical treatment and had been sexually assaulted in the rehabilitation facilities, and they showed it again, to United Nations staff and international human rights groups, just a few weeks later in Mexico City at the 17th International AIDS Conference. APNSW received awards for their work exposing the abuses driven by US policy, which itself remains the same.

The day I visited the brothel in Phnom Penh was just a few months before the worst of the US-influenced crackdowns would begin. The brothel grounds and the road leading to it were covered in dust, which left red dirt on the bottom of my laptop bag when I sat it down to take a seat on one of the plastic chairs between the bungalow-like buildings. I didn't take any photos. It was just a moment to breathe in the place, the smell of diesel fuel and the sounds of multiple televisions playing against each other and drifting out into the night air. Everything that was necessary to me about this place was in the stories I had already heard, on the boat, on the outreach van, off the clock.

Before I left Phnom Penh, WNU hosted a musical revue, with burlesque, karaoke, and traditional dance. The Condi/Bush video played on a big screen, and a sex worker activist from Fiji lip-synched as Mary Magdalene, dressed in business drag and wearing pearls.

10

The Movement

When prostitutes win, all women win.

      —Black Women for Wages for Housework (1977)

COYOTE Howls was the newsletter of the first prostitutes' rights organization in the United States. It was published from San Francisco in the latter half of the seventies, and like any good alternative newspaper of the time, it had a robust back-of-the-paper section with classified listings. But being a newsletter for and by whores, the back pages advertised their own satellite organizations. There were the Prostitutes Union of Massachusetts (PUMA), the Spread Eagles (Washington, DC), the Kansas City Kitties (Missouri), Scapegoat (New York), and PROWL (Professional Resource Organization for Women's Liberties; Spokane, Washington). The copy of *COYOTE Howls* on my desk now (lent from the archives of legendary sex worker activist Carol Leigh) bears the headline "Hookers and Housewives Come Together: Violence Abortion Welfare Become Common Issues at 1977 International Women's Year Conference."

"Hookers and Housewives." It's hard now to conceive of these groups of women as class allies. Hookers and housewives, to speak in impossible generalities, are too often considered rivals (by those on the Left as much as by those on the Right), occupying opposite sides of one economic circle, two classes of women who earn their living from men's waged work. Their labor, by contrast, is considered illegitimate. Caretaking and sex should be offered freely, we're told, with genuine affection and out of love. A housewife maintains her legitimacy by not seeking a wage, and a hooker breaks with convention by demanding one. They are both diminished and confined by the same system that would keep women dependent on men for survival. And they could free themselves from that system together.

As Margo St. James recalled in an interview (also from Carol Leigh's archives), before she founded COYOTE in early 1973, there was WHO—Whores, Housewives, and Others. Others meant lesbians, "but it wasn't being said out loud yet, even in liberal bohemian circles." An early COYOTE supporter, anthropologist Jennifer James, coined the term "decriminalization" to express the movement's goals of removing laws used to target prostitutes. The National Organization for Women (NOW), still very much in its *Feminine Mystique* era, adopted the decriminalization of prostitution as an official part of its platform later that year.

Feminist thinker Wendy McElroy wrote in her essay "Prostitutes, Feminists and Economic Associates" that to the early prostitutes' rights movement the feminist movement reacted with applause. *Ms.* magazine lauded both the efforts and the personality of Margo St. James. As late as 1979, prostitutes and mainstream feminists were actively cooperating. For example, COYOTE aligned with NOW in what was called a "Kiss and Tell" campaign to further the ERA [Equal Rights Amendment] effort.

McElroy cites a 1979 issue of *COYOTE Howls*, which reads:

COYOTE has called on all prostitutes to join the international "Kiss and Tell" campaign to convince legislators that it is in their best interest to support . . . issues of importance to women. The organizers of the campaign are urging that the names of legislators who have consistently voted against those issues, yet are regular patrons of prostitutes, be turned over to feminist organizations for their use.

It's as optimistic as it was naive, if you could have looked ahead to what became the highest-profile political sex work scandal in the United States. Eliot Spitzer was the prochoice Democrat from New York who as New York State attorney general targeted corruption on Wall Street and as governor signed legislation toughening prostitution penalties that could have been used against him had he not stepped down first, slunk off, and waited the requisite months before launching himself back into the public sphere, as men like him often do. In the United States, anyway, a right-wing politician opposed to women's rights, such as Louisiana's Republican senator David Vitter, can turn up on an escort agency's client list and be elected to another term. Is it that conservatives harbor less shame, or that liberals possess no spine with which to support sex workers while actually in office—or both?

Just two years after COYOTE's formation, in June 1975, more than one hundred prostitutes occupied the Saint-Nizier Church in Lyon, France. The action inspired other French prostitutes to occupy churches in their own cities in solidarity with those in Lyon, who held Saint-Nizier for ten days before being evicted by police with force. In Lyon, feminist groups grappled with how—or if—to support the occupying prostitutes. A feminist leaflet from the time, translated by Lilian Mathieu, reads:

> We, like they, are in the situation of prostitutes, in that, forced to marry, we are obliged to sell ourselves body and soul to our lord and master in order to survive and have a respectable place in this male society.

Though the feminists who supported the prostitutes ultimately wished to end the practice of prostitution, "by presenting the movement as 'the symbol of the liberation of all women,'" writes Lilian Mathieu in the essay "An Unlikely Mobilization," quoting another leaflet, "the feminists tried to universalize, or expand, the cause they had seized on, and thereby to legitimate it."

"They justified their solidarity," he continues, by claiming, as one of their leaflets went, that "'it's not just on the street that women are led to prostitute themselves.'" Lyon's prostitutes, like those in New York crashing feminist conferences nearly concurrently, could see this support was outrageously conditional.

There's a photo inside the 1977 "Hookers and Housewives" edition, a near-perfect illustration of the headline, of Margo St. James standing before a mic on the steps of San Francisco's city hall with three unnamed members of Wages for Housework (another emergent force in the late seventies' women's movement, who went on to support the London church occupation by the English Collective of Prostitutes), two black women and one white woman. One woman holds a sign, AMNESTY FOR ALL PROSTITUTES. Had this image of feminism found its way to me before any of those now iconic shots of that more ubiquitous icon of seventies feminism, Gloria Steinem, so often seated solo, indoors, with her highlighted hair in its center-part, those tinted glasses that dwarfed her face, I could have paired Steinem's with another: a feminism both of and for the streets. The caption under the photo reads:

> May 9th demonstration by Wages for Housework protesting violence against women. Moments later, [Margo St. James] was yanked, headfirst, down the steps, by her hair. It took 14 phone calls to get the D.A. to press charges against the man who committed the unprovoked assault.

By the time I arrived in San Francisco thirty years after COYOTE's founding, having moved into an apartment just behind City Hall, Margo St. James had left for Europe, and then again for rural Washington State. Her name was a continued presence in sex workers' rights circles, including in the naming of a clinic—the St. James Infirmary—founded in her honor. I moved to San Francisco in 2003 because that's where the movement was. Really, it was where all the movements were: Without its student liberation movement, its black liberation movement, its women's liberation movement, and its gay liberation movement I can't imagine San Francisco birthing a prostitutes' rights movement from a houseboat docked in Sausalito, where Margo herself had lived.

But before Margo St. James, there was Sylvia Rivera, who took her place in history at the Stonewall riots. In the same year that Margo formed COYOTE Sylvia was intervening in one of the first Gay Freedom Day celebrations, in Washington Square Park. You can watch her yourself, in a film discovered and posted online by transgender activist Reina Gossett. "Y'all better quiet down!" she yells, her voice even when amplified straining over the boos from the crowd. "I've been trying to get up here all day for your gay brothers and your gay sisters in jail." Today as many as a third of transgender people in the United States have been incarcerated at some time in their lives. "Most of these women are not in jail for violent crimes," says transgender activist and author Janet Mock "it's for survival work." That is: for the crime of refusing poverty, for hustling or trading sex. How many people could we spare prison, I want to know, if we simply stopped arresting people for selling sex?

This is how it came to pass, after fighting the police at Stonewall and putting gay liberation on the national map, that Sylvia Rivera had to fight to speak at the anniversary of that riot. Radical lesbians in the gay movement had denounced transgender women like Rivera as "female impersonators," accusing them of profiting off of women's oppression. "The transgender community was silenced because of a radical lesbian named Jean O'Leary," Sylvia Rivera recalled,

> who felt that the transgender community was offensive to women because we liked to wear makeup and we liked to wear miniskirts. Excuse me! It goes with the business that we're in at the time! No we do not. We don't want to be out there sucking dick and getting fucked in the ass. But that's the only alternative that we have to survive because the laws do not give us the right to go and get a job the way we feel comfortable. I do not want to go to work looking like a man when I know I am not a man.

It was Sylvia who stood up for the trans women and queer kids who ended up in jail when they hustled and did sex work to get by. Rivera did sex work, too, to take care of herself and to raise money for the organizing project and shelter she started with Marsha P. Johnson, called STAR (Street Transvestite Action Revolutionaries), the first transgender organization in the United States. They were harassed by the police even when they weren't hustling, just for being visible. The police raids on bars such as Stonewall were written up as "vice raids" in the press, when laws against cross-dressing or two men or two women dancing together fell under that rubric. The police enforced their outcast status and, as with every outcast group, did so along the lines of who they already considered most suspect.

On a warm night in June 2011, when same-sex marriage

was legalized in New York State, it would be hard to imagine the cops breaking up the giant party that followed at Stonewall in Greenwich Village, and in the streets outside. But a few blocks north, in the building that houses the community law project named for Sylvia Rivera, cops had been conducting surveillance, stopping queer and trans youth of color coming and going and asking them to name the young trans women in photographs they had printed off.

Recalling those years just before Stonewall and not long before prostitutes' rights became a national issue too, author and activist Amber Hollibaugh writes in her essay collection *My Dangerous Desires*:

> I was a United Farm Workers organizer. I belonged to two communes, snuck desperate men trying to escape the Vietnam War across the Canadian border, marched in protest against the Vietnam War in cities all over the country, laid in front of Black Panther offices late at night to keep police from firing inside, and got my first tear gas mask at eighteen to use in the street riots that I regularly joined. Then, late at night, I did sex work. Prostitution made it possible for me to afford an existence most middle-class and upper-middle-class radicals I knew assumed was inherently theirs by right.

Amber Hollibaugh, Sylvia Rivera, and Marsha P. Johnson are far from alone in funding movement work with sex work. I think back, too, on those people I met in the sex workers' rights movement in San Francisco, thirty years after COYOTE's formation, who were using sex work to support their unpaid activist work. Those who had laid the groundwork for the movement in the eighties and nineties were, by that time, more or less retired from sex work. They didn't come up the way this new generation came up, the Reagan babies and Clinton kids, who got our start in the business just as the first wave of sex worker chic hit with feminism's third wave. Our generation had never known a world before AIDS, had only vague memories of a sex industry before the Internet. We didn't have the sexual revolution; we had decades of sex panic.

We weren't wholly reliant on the Internet to become politicized. It was my AIDS activism in the mid- and late nineties that introduced me to queer politics, to sex workers' rights— all of a mix. One spring we marched in the streets of Boston for the rights of queer youth; the next spring, before the official youth pride march, the only other out queer woman in my high school, who had been running with the Lesbian Avengers, pulled me into a smaller unpermitted march along a desolate section of Massachusetts Avenue, being held in memory of a trans woman who had been doing sex work and was murdered. The cops had done nothing. Maybe this is what united us, these movements: We kept coming together, each in our own ways, against the assumed inevitability of our early deaths.

So we were never one movement, even if together we had— in books such as *Whores and Other Feminists* and documentaries such as *Live Nude Girls Unite!*—begun to tell its story.

A week or two after taking the apartment behind San Francisco's City Hall, I heard about the arrest, across the bay in Berkeley, of a woman named Shannon Williams, who had been working out of an apartment when it was stormed by over a dozen police in heavy gear, with weapons drawn, all to charge her with a 647b, the California state criminal law against solicitation. I had made one of my first new San Francisco friends online, and she was a sex worker and massage therapist. She volunteered at St. James Infirmary by giving free massages as part of its occupational safety drop-in clinic every Wednesday. The infirmary didn't just offer HIV tests and condoms, but also primary and holistic health care, and all of it for free. M. and I were hanging out in her apartment in Oakland, and she was telling me about this protest she heard a new group was putting on. Shannon Williams had been arrested while wearing leopard-print lingerie, and the police hadn't let her get dressed before they cuffed her and walked her to the cop car, so the protesters were going to wear leopard print when they stood outside the courthouse for her arraignment. That group became Sex Workers Outreach Project–USA. Williams's arrest launched a new wave of sex worker advocacy across the country.

SWOP–USA gathered again in San Francisco in December 2003, on the patch of grass at the foot of the steps of City Hall, to hold a vigil for forty-eight victims of violence. After twenty years, a married, middle-aged, white man had finally confessed to killing these women in the Pacific Northwest. Gary Leon Ridgway, the Green River Killer, said:

> I picked prostitutes as my victims because I hate most prostitutes and I did not want to pay them for sex. I also picked prostitutes as victims because they were easy to

pick up without being noticed. I knew they would not be reported missing right away and might never be reported missing. I picked prostitutes because I thought I could kill as many of them as I wanted without getting caught.

He told police:

I thought I was doing you guys a favor, killing prostitutes. Here you guys can't control them, but I can.

Annie Sprinkle, an artist, former prostitute and porn star, and one of the first wave of sex worker activists in the seventies and eighties, had proposed there be a vigil. Sex workers needed a way to remember those deaths and to speak out against the culture of catastrophic and outrageous neglect that makes them vulnerable to violence, and to protest against the cops who had looked the other way except to arrest them. Women's groups were always speaking out against rape and violence, as with the marches through San Francisco's red-light districts that Carol Leigh had reacted to twenty-five years before when she coined the phrase "sex work." This was our turn. Sex Workers Outreach Project–USA had come together to support the Berkeley teacher arrested in her leopard-print lingerie and now ran with the vigil, making it an annual Day to End Violence Against Sex Workers observance. It had a not uncomplicated relationship to the establishment women's groups, which rarely supported us in public. A feminist antiprostitution group tried unsuccessfully to disrupt the vigil in its second year. In its sixth year, after that antiprostitution group's founder had passed away from cancer, we remembered her at the vigil, too. And in the tenth year of the vigil, after SWOP–USA's cofounder, Robyn Few, passed away from cancer, there were dozens of observances around the world recognizing her and her fight.

It can't all be death and loss, though, even if sometimes the joy in the movement—the karaoke, PVC, leopard print, and all—makes sex workers seem unfit for "real" politics. Who else would use a fashion show of streetwalker chic to protest a little understood US policy restricting foreign aid to groups who oppose prostitution? But that's what Brazilian sex workers from the organization Daspu asked sex workers to help them do onstage at the International AIDS Conference in Mexico City in 2008. Daspu members gave SWOP–USA members catwalk makeovers, and before an audience of UN people and the international human rights crowd, they used boots, fishnets, and smoky eyes to tell their story: The groups had been strong-armed by the US into signing loyalty oaths declaring their opposition to prostitution in order to keep their AIDS funds. Rather than sell out sex workers, the entire country of Brazil refused to sign the pledge and gave up $40 million.

On another cold night in December, almost ten years after SWOP's founding, we gathered again, but this time lit by a stage and not candles, not mourning but organizing. Members of SWOP–NYC were raising money to spin off PERSIST, a health project for those in the sex trade. It was inspired by the St. James Infirmary, and brought more than a hundred people together, crammed into that sweaty little room in their best drag, to bid on spankings and T-shirts. We applauded performer after performer, and got choked up and misty when the organizers hopped onstage to thank us—and then got back to cruising and mingling and dancing, a mix of generations, some back again at the Stonewall Inn.

Not long after that benefit at Stonewall I interviewed one of the health project's cofounders, Sarah Elspeth Patterson, for a story in anticipation of their launch. After the ten years since SWOP was founded, the forty years since COYOTE and STAR were founded, the movement was beginning to resemble those roots again. I would find sex workers' rights activists on the streets of Lower Manhattan when I was reporting on Occupy Wall Street, marching but also lending expertise in street medicine, in harm reduction, in jail support, all the things sex workers had learned to care for themselves outside the law.

At a community meeting that winter at Riverside Church near Harlem, about the NYPD's policy of stop-and-frisk, a group of trans women, all Latina, came to the mic one after the other and described in Spanish how they had been targeted by the police: stopped while walking home from the subway or stopped when buying a cup of coffee (and an instance when one woman asked the officer why she was being stopped, she had the coffee thrown in her face). They said they were profiled as sex workers, whether they were working or not, and had the condoms in their purses used as evidence of their intent to do sex work.

When the International AIDS Conference finally returned to the United States in the summer of 2012, after the ban on HIV-positive people entering the United States had been lifted, the travel ban on sex workers and drug users remained. Two of the groups recognized as most at-risk were shut out of the gathering, the largest in the world to address AIDS, to set policy goals and funding commitments. In the streets of Washington, DC, a few dozen American sex workers marched as a contingent in a larger march against the criminalization of AIDS. Something in the movement was shifting back: a recognition that, as destructive as the laws that target prostitution are, they are applied to us unequally, and to many more people than sex workers.

> One thing I want everyone to understand is that when ppl scream abt how empowering [sex work] is, they are reacting directly to whorephobia. It does not mean our work is abt sex rather than economics. It means you have left them no room for a complicated relationship with work or any possible other paradigms. Sex work can indeed be empowering. But that is not the point. Money is the fucking point.
> —Kitty Carr

A movement that had in some ways been founded on the principles of sexual liberation, and had found itself pitted against feminists, was focusing now not on why sex is outlawed but why sex is a vehicle by which people are made outlaws. It's not only a movement to reclaim the value of sex, though it is that and would lose its sense of joy and life without that, but it is also a movement to reject the systems that use sex to render certain people less valuable.

Some of this has been accomplished by placing less emphasis on sex work as the banner under which the movement is organized. When she co-founded PERSIST Sarah Elspeth

Patterson told me that it was important *not* to describe the people who run it and the community it serves as sex workers, not out of shame or stigma, but to address all the people who are involved in their own way in the sex trade and do not use that word to describe themselves. It can look like a disavowal of a foundational element of sex worker movement work, but it comes from the same place the phrase sex worker originated from: the power built in naming yourself.

"Sex worker," Patterson pointed out, isn't a term that most sex workers use in the course of their actual work. They don't advertise themselves that way; they're escorts, or rent boys, or massage providers, or porn performers, or dommes, or subs, or simply working girls. Sex workers do use the name in their organizing, in their political work. But they've constructed a class identity as workers that they can't use at work.

There's one critical function sex worker identity must still perform: It gives shape to the demand that sex workers are as defined by their work as they are by their sexuality; it de-eroticizes the public perception of the sex worker, not despite sex but to force recognition of sex workers outside of a sexual transaction.

Our political work is still understood as sex, as if we cannot speak without producing pornography. I think of the men who come to my public talks, who corner me with personal questions about my "real work" after I've given a reading or delivered a lecture on my reporting or research. I recall my file of e-mails from reporters, academics, filmmakers, and activists who want me to introduce them to sex workers so that they can tell their stories, or organize them, without an understanding that they—we—are also reporters, academics, filmmakers, and activists, and are doing it ourselves. After I repeatedly told one such person that I couldn't meet with him to discuss his "research," he then asked me out for a drink, not realizing that if he wants this kind of interaction from a sex worker, he could just hire one who was actually working.

There has to be a way to embrace sex worker identity without finding ourselves expected, again and again, to perform someone else's sexual fantasy, whether they come dressed as a jailer or a comrade. But at the same time, our politics cannot deny the body just because someone else has a complex about it.

Whore Solidarity

I don't know that we'll ever have enough of a mass of people who have done sex work who want to reclaim the word *whore*— as some have done with the word *queer*—but there is a vocal group who do, and most of the time I would join them. Let's say we do, though, for the same reasons that some of us also call ourselves dykes (even if and when we fuck men for money): to drain some of the hate off this word, to take up a little more space for ourselves in the world and to do it without shame, to resist all the times and ways we've been labeled by people who are not us. The reclamation, as these things always are, will be uneven. People in our own community will think it's a bad idea, or bad for us, and some of us will do it anyway.

I don't know that using the word *whore* to describe yourself takes anything away from anyone. Just stating that no one else's value is robbed by whatever it is that's happening between my legs, and whatever it is I have to say about it, is precisely why it might be important to take *whore* back.

Maybe it's too late for that. Maybe, in the early decades of the twenty-first century, we no longer make political acts out of repurposing stigmatizing labels when we're supposed to have left things like identity politics back in the dust of the nineties, along with our flannels, fishnets, and Foucault. But "all politics are identity politics," as *Jacobin* magazine editor Peter Frase put it in his essay "An Imagined Community," and besides, "as post-modern, ironic subjects, we will be unable to avoid facing the artificiality of our identities."

So *whore* isn't something to be abandoned entirely, like those fashions or those arguments, as just some form of fashionable political drag. By speaking it we are bringing it forward in history, along with ourselves. "To appropriate the past uncritically," Frase concludes, "would be to exclude all those who were excluded in the past." Coming together around all the markers of who we are—where we come from, how we work, who we fuck—is how we produce the possibility of solidarity, no matter what we call it.

I imagine what solidarity with whores would look like.

Because so long as there are women who are called whores, there will be women who are trained to believe it is next to death to be one or to be mistaken for one. And so long as that is, men will feel they can leave whores for dead with impunity. The fear of the whore, or of being the whore, is the engine that drives the whole thing. That engine could be called "misogyny," but even that word misses something: the cheapness of the whore, how easily she might be discarded not only due to her gender but to her race, her class. Whore is maybe the original intersectional insult.

To build a class on this moves us away from our perception of the whore as someone endangered principally by patriarchy to someone whose body is crossed by multiple points of prejudice and violence—oppression and exploitation not in the abstract hands of men but in the specific institutions that prop them up. Some lines are more legible than others. Some create borders—white woman, successful white woman—that others stake their whole politics on maintaining. But to us living where they cross, we resist being defined by these borders alone, even as we are seen through them.

This is how we could reimagine whore as a class. Because it's not just that laws against prostitution make the act of selling sex illegal; it's that laws against prostitution are used to target a class of people as whores whether or not they are selling sex, and in areas of their lives far outside what they do for a living.

In recognition of this, it is fair to say that there are multiple sex worker movements. The sex worker rights movement has its own character, history, and trajectory. But there are many more sex workers in movements that are not specifically called sex workers' movements: in queer and trans movements, in radical women-of-color movements, in harm-reduction organizing, in the prison abolition movement. In welfare women's movements. In migrants' movements. In labor movements. You just have to know where to look.

And in feminist movements. As hard as some feminists work to exclude sex workers, it's the sex worker feminists who keep me coming back to feminism.

There's two distinct but overlapping strands of activism within the movement for sex workers' rights. One is concerned with changing the conditions of the sex trade itself. Its internal campaigns focus on improving workplace conditions, on workers' rights. Its external campaigns target institutions outside sex work that impact sex workers—and police and health care providers are highest on that list. The other strand is primarily concerned with changing conditions outside the trade to impact the lives of people who do and who used to do sex work, or people who are profiled as sex workers. The first strand, which is more vocally identified with sex workers' rights, may be more likely to argue for decriminalization in policy and building the political power of current sex workers to control the terms of their work. The second strand, which may not outwardly identify as a sex workers' rights movement, may be more likely to argue for an end to criminalization as it's experienced in its community's daily life, and in building the capacity of current and former sex workers individually and collectively to define their own lives. These strands of the movement converge and go their own ways, but their common purpose is to value and believe the experiences of people who sell sex, to insist that it is not sex work that degrades us but those people who use our experiences to justify degradation.

Outside the United States, where some sex workers' movements emerged aligned much more closely with labor, health and human rights causes than feminist movements, these strands might look quite different. To an extent, necessity has bred an intersectional movement, one that offers the potential for so many connections: to migrants' rights, to informal and excluded workers' organizing. To the degree that sex workers can find safer spaces to come out in other movements, those connections can be fostered into something powerful. And to the degree that stigma and criminalization makes that frightening, sex workers will be more occupied fighting for survival alone than in finding solidarity.

Solidarity—not support. This is what's absent in even well-meaning "support" for sex workers: a willingness to direct that support at those people who have the power to change anything about the conditions of sex workers' lives.

And this is where we lose: endless, circular conversations about how sex work makes you feel (if you are someone who has not done it) that serve only to stand in for taking action. Your feelings about sex work do not make much difference to the vice police working tonight. Be bolder and look closer to home. And if you must have your feelings, take them to people who will listen: neighborhood associations, health clinics, labor unions, domestic violence shelters, queer and women's organizations—your own people, whoever they are. Rather than narrow in on sex workers' behaviors, turn your questions outward. What are these people doing that might harm sex workers? Why not help *them*, rather than sex workers, change their behavior?

Just as suspect as too much feelings talk is the impulse from those who have never done sex work to offer up their own standards by which they wish it was regulated. For people who have never so much as talked about taking their clothes off for money they have a lot of ideas about how others should do so. What is needed long before any kind of proposals for sex industry regulation can be made is a recognition that under criminalization, sex work *is* regulated—by the criminal and legal system, by cops. Even for sex workers who work independently and without any kind of management, cops *are* management.

The first step in talking about meaningful standards for sex work is to make space for sex workers to lead that process. That will not happen so long as law enforcement are on sex workers' backs.

Likewise, sex workers don't want others rushing in, however well meaning, to be the new boss. Sex workers are used to being excluded from developing the policies that rule their lives. Here are a few I've heard most often, and from all political corners, that continue to miss the point.

- *If only it were legal, we could tax them.* Which ignores all the taxes currently paid by sex workers on their income and on what they purchase.
- *If only it were legal, we could test them.* Never mind that sex workers already have an economic interest in maintaining their sexual health, that STI and HIV rates among sex workers have more to do with their ability to negotiate safe sex (itself constrained under criminalization) than with how many partners they have. Or that the global health community considers mandatory HIV testing to cause people to avoid health professionals,

increasing their health risks. And that by the standards set forth by UNAIDS and the International Labor Organization, forcing someone—no matter what their occupation is—to be tested for HIV is considered a violation of human rights.

- *If only it were legal, we could register them.* You might say we expect such protocols of other businesses, but as a culture we have yet to dignify sex work as any other business. Forced registration just looks like policing by a different name to sex workers. Those who refuse to register will form a new underground.

None of these proposals—even if they weren't so foolish—are mine to make. It's not my job, and besides, I'm not sure we're ready if we can't yet answer one question: In what way do any of these proposals serve sex workers?

Here's my only proposal, because it is long overdue: If only sex work were not criminal, sex workers could do so much more for themselves, and for each other. But why should we wait?

There's no reason to wait for all these attitudes to change, for whore stigma to somehow fall away, to make room for another way, whether that's amending the law, ending sex workers' status as outlaws by other means, or by something more and yet unimagined. To hope that all those others who are occupied by their obsession with us—by the prostitutes in their fantasies—to wait for them to change and accept sex work as work and sex workers as full agents in their own lives before we take the lead? They won't. It's through our demands, our imaginations, that we will.

Acknowledgements

Thanks to the excellent editorial staff at Verso who shaped this book, especially Audrea Lim and Angelica Sgouros. Thanks to the *Jacobin* crew and to publisher Bhaskar Sunkara, for bringing this into their inaugural book series.

To all those who made a home for me in San Francisco, where this book began ten years ago: Gina de Vries, Naomi Akers, Sadie Lune, Stacey Swimme, Sarah Dopp, thank you. Thank you to friends with the Exotic Dancers' Union, to family at St. James Infirmary. To Carol Leigh, for her imagination and her commitment, and for lending me a piece of history in COYOTE's archives, thank you.

To my dedicated former colleagues at the Third Wave Foundation, who refused to back away from sex workers' rights and freedom, thank you, and thank you for introducing me to the work of many of the incredible activists I draw on every day.

To the sex worker writers, organizers, late night comrades, and legends—Audacia Ray, Charlotte Shane, Susan Elizabeth Shepard, Darby Hickey, everyone from #sexworktwitter I haven't been lucky enough to meet yet—thank you for keeping me going and keeping me up.

Thanks to Caty Simon, for more than a decade of friendship and sharp thinking that shaped this right from the start.

Thanks of the highest order, and also whiskey, to fierce friends and first readers, Sarah Jaffe and Joanne McNeil.

With love, thanks to Tommy Moore, for endless encouragement, for cake, for the home that held this, for agreeing that the Nick Cave epigraph I was on the fence about was best kept between us.

Further Reading

Encyclopedia of Prostitution and Sex Work. Melissa Hope Ditmore, ed. (Greenwood Publishing Group: 2006)

Global Sex Workers: Rights, Resistance, and Redefinition. Kamala Kempadoo, Jo Doezema, eds. (Routledge: 1998)

Flesh for Fantasy: Producing and Consuming Exotic Dance. R. Danielle Egan, Katherine Frank, Merri Lisa Johnson, eds. (Seal Press: 2005)

Indecent: How I Fake It and Make It As A Girl For Hire. Sarah Katherine Lewis (Seal Press: 2006)

The Last of the Live Nude Girls: A Memoir. Sheila McClear (Soft Skull Press: 2011)

The Little Black Book of Grisélidis Réal: Days and Nights of an Anarchist Whore. Jean-Luc Henning; Ariana Reines, trans. (semiotext(e): 2009)

Live Sex Acts: Women Performing Erotic Labor. Wendy Chapkis (Routledge: 1996)

The Lost Sisterhood: Prostitution in America 1900–1918. Ruth Rosen (Johns Hopkins University Press: 1983)

My Dangerous Desires: A Queer Girl Dreaming Her Way Home. Amber L. Hollibaugh (Duke University Press: 2000)

Naked on the Internet: Hookups, Downloads, and Cashing in on Internet Sexploration. Audacia Ray (Seal Press: 2007)

Policing Pleasure: Sex Work, Policy, and the State in Global Perspective. Susan Dewey, Patty Kelly, eds. (New York University Press: 2011)

Queer (In)justice: The Criminalization of LGBT People in the United States. Joey L. Mogul, Andrea J. Ritchie, Kay Whitlock, eds. (Beacon Press: 2011)

Race, Sex, and Class: The Perspective of Winning, A Selection of Writings 1952–2011. Selma James (PM Press: 2012)

Real Live Nude Girl: Chronicles of Sex-Positive Culture. Carol Queen (Cleis Press: 1997)

Reading, Writing, and Rewriting the Prostitute Body. Shannon Bell (Indiana University Press: 1994)

Rent Girl. Michelle Tea and Laurenn McCubbin (Last Gasp: 2004)

Prose and Lore: Memoir Stories About Sex Work, vols. 1–3. Audacia Ray, ed. (Red Umbrella Project)

Sex at the Margins: Migration, Labour Markets and the Rescue Industry. Laura María Agustín (Zed Books: 2007)

Sex Slaves and Discourse Masters: The Construction of Trafficking. Jo Doezema (Zed Books: 2010)

Sex Work: Writings by Women in the Sex Industry. Frédérique Delacoste, Priscilla Alexander, eds. (Cleis Press: 1998)

Sex Work Matters: Exploring Money, Power, and Intimacy in the Sex Industry. Melissa Hope Ditmore, Antonia Levy, Alys Willman, eds. (Zed Books: 2010)

Sex Workers Unite: A History of the Movement from Stonewall to SlutWalk, Melinda Chateauvert (Beacon Press: 2014)

The State of Sex: Tourism, Sex and Sin in the New American Heartland. Barbara G. Brents, Crystal A. Jackson, and Kathryn Hausbeck (Routledge: 2009)

"State Violence, Sex Trade, and the Failure of Anti-Trafficking Policies." Emi Koyama (eminism.org, 2013)

Strip City: A Stripper's Farewell Journey Across America. Lily Burana (Miramax: 2003)

St. James Infirmary: Occupational Health and Safety Handbook, Third Edition. (stjamesinfirmary.org, 2010)

Temporarily Yours: Intimacy, Authenticity, and the Commerce of Sex. Elizabeth Bernstein (University of Chicago Press: 2010)

"A Theory of Violence: In Honor of Kasandra, CeCe, Savita, and Anonymous." Eesha Pandit (Crunk Feminist Collective, January 4, 2013)

Unrepentant Whore: The Collected Works of Scarlot Harlot. Carol Leigh (Last Gasp Books: 2004)

Whores and Other Feminists. Jill Nagle, ed. (Routledge: 1997)

Working Sex: Sex Workers Write About a Changing Industry. Annie Oakley, ed. (Seal Press: 2008)